Touring the Globe
Through Sounds and Scenes

MUSIC+TRAVEL

WORLDWIDE

MUSEYON
GUIDES

A CURATED GUIDE TO YOUR OBSESSIONS

www.museyon.com

©Museyon, Inc. 2009

Publisher: Akira Chiba
Editors: Anne Ishii, Stef Schwalb
Art Director: Eriko Ito
Sales and Marketing Manager: Laura Robinson
Managing Editor, museyon.com: Heather Corcoran

Cover Photo ©fimkaJane
Cover Illustration: ©Jillian Tamaki copyright 2009

Published in the United States by:
Museyon, Inc.
20 E. 46th St. Ste. 1400
New York, NY 10017

ISBN 978-0-9822320-3-3

021062

Printed in China

RMANY

RUSSIA

CHINA

INDIA

TURKEY

ETHIOPIA

AUSTRALIA

TABLE OF CONTENTS

01 : JAZZ LAND   8

UNITED STATES - CHICAGO
BY PETER MARGASAK

Timeline   8
Before You Go, Get in the Know   10
Hometown Heroes   12
Influential Chicago Jazz Albums   14
Art Imitating Life: The Music in Movies   16
See it for Yourself   18
Map of Venues and City Landmarks   22

02 : BRING THE NOISE, BRING THE PUNK   24

IRELAND - DUBLIN
BY JAMES HENDICOTT

Timeline   24
Before You Go, Get in the Know   27
Hometown Heroes   28
Albums That Influenced Celtic Punk Rock in Dublin   30
See it for Yourself   36
Map of Venues and City Landmarks   38

03 : NEW RAP CITY   40

FRANCE - PARIS
BY MILES MARSHALL LEWIS

Timeline   40
Before You Go, Get in the Know   43
Hometown Heroes   44
Art Imitating Life: The Music in Movies   45
Albums That Influenced Muslim Hip-Hop in Paris   46
Map of Venues and City Landmarks   54

04 : TECHNO COLOR   56

GERMANY - BERLIN
BY SIOBHAN O'LEARY

Timeline   56
Before You Go, Get in the Know   58
Hometown Heroes   60
Albums That Influenced Techno in Berlin   62
Art Imitating Life: The Music in Movies   65
See it for Yourself   66
Map of Venues and City Landmarks   68

05 : JAILHOUSE ROCK 70
RUSSIA - MOSCOW + ST. PETERSBURG
BY ALINA SIMONE

Timeline 70
Before You Go, Get in the Know 72
Hometown Heroes 74
See it for Yourself 75
Albums That Influenced Chanson in Moscow + St. Petersburg 76
Map of Venues and City Landmarks 84

06 : CLASSICAL STUDIES 86
TURKEY - ISTANBUL
BY ALEXANDRA IVANOFF

Timeline 86
Before You Go, Get in the Know 88
Hometown Heroes 90
On Location: Istanbul Classical Music Scene 91
Albums That Influenced Classical Music in Istanbul 92
See it for Yourself 98
Map of Venues and City Landmarks 100

07 : SWING SHIFTS 102
ETHIOPIA - ADDIS ABABA
BY MIKAEL AWAKE

Timeline 102
Before You Go, Get in the Know 105
Hometown Heroes 106
Albums That Influenced Ethiopop in Ethiopia 108
See it for Yourself 114
Map of Venues and City Landmarks 116

08 : PASSAGE TO INDIPOP 118
INDIA - MUMBAI
BY SHAMIK BAG

Timeline 118
Before You Go, Get in the Know 120
Hometown Heroes 122
Influential Indipop Albums in Mumbai 124
See it for Yourself 130
Map of Venues and City Landmarks 132

TABLE OF CONTENTS

09 : EXPERIMENTAL METHODS   134

CHINA - BEIJING
BY NICK FRISCH

Timeline	134
Before You Go, Get in the Know	136
Hometown Heroes	138
Landmark Albums of Experimental Music in Beijing	140
See it for Yourself	146
Map of Venues and City Landmarks	148

10 : ART ROCK CONFIDENTIAL   150

AUSTRALIA - MELBOURNE, SYDNEY + BRISBANE
BY MEL CAMPBELL

Timeline	150
Before You Go, Get in the Know	153
Hometown Heroes	154
Albums That Influenced Art Rock in Australia	156
See it for Yourself	162
Map of Venues and City Landmarks	164

11 : THE DIGITAL DOMAIN   166

ARGENTINA - BUENOS AIRES
BY EVE HYMAN

Timeline	166
Before You Go, Get in the Know	169
Hometown Heroes	170
Albums That Influence Cumbia in Buenos Aires	172
Building Your Own Collection	176
Map of Venues and City Landmarks	180

12 : FOLK LURE   182

UNITED STATES - SOUTHERN CALIFORNIA
BY JESSICA HUNDLEY

Timeline	182
Before You Go, Get in the Know	184
Hometown Heroes	186
See it for Yourself	187
Albums That Influenced Calicountry in the LA Area	188
Side Roads and Sister Cities	190
Calicountry Today	192
Map of Venues and City Landmarks	194

INDEX + CREDITS: DISCOGRAPHY, FESTIVALS, CONTRIBUTORS AND ACKNOWLEDGEMENTS   196-207

Everybody's done it –played air guitar in a bar, busted a move in your bedroom, or sang with power in the shower. No matter what the genre, no matter who the musician, no matter where we are, music moves us.

It's inspiring and infectious, and easily one of life's greatest pleasures to obsess over. Devoted followers will stand in the rain for hours to get a ticket to their concert of choice, or drop everything if offered access to their favorite artist. The staff here at Museyon Guides know how you feel—we've done it ourselves.

It's also why we've created this book. Because not only do we love to listen to music—we love to learn about it. Historical origins, artists' influences, landmark albums are what tie so many musical genres together. It's the crossover that helps you expand your musical horizons. Sharing music has been a favorite pastime of fans long before MySpace, iTunes, and last.fm (those outlets have just helped speed up the process). So what better way to gain more musical knowledge and appreciation then to head to the cities where specific genres have staked their claim?

We enlisted 12 writers in 12 different countries to put their knowledge and aural addiction to work as a force for good, and give you the inside skinny on the sounds and scenes of some of the coolest genres around the globe as a result. Some of these include cumbia in Buenos Aires, Celtic punk in Dublin, chanson in Moscow and St. Petersburg, and classical in Istanbul. You'll also discover the origins of Muslim hip-hop in Paris, the Berlin clubs that keep the beats of techno pumping, which Chicago jazz musicians are keeping the genre jumping, and more.

Because we believe that music makes the world go round—or at the least, makes it sound a lot sweeter.

01: JAZZ LAND

by Peter Margasak

1920s ▶▶▶

New Orleans-born jazz incubates in Chicago with migration of black Southerners northward.

1950s ▶▶▶

Hard bop flourishes in Chicago while jazz musicians start migrating further east to New York.

1960s ▶▶▶

Local economy collapses. Taverns and bars replace regular musicians with DJs. The Association for the Advancement of Creative Musicians (AACM) emerges out of unemployment.

1990s-2000s

Reedist Ken Vandermark leads the explosion of current Chicago jazz fervor, and for over 15 years the city has been known as the top place for experimentation and hard-nose playing.

Lake Michigan

Chicago ●

Chicago River at Night photo: ©Jim Jurica

Segal's Jazz Showcase
photo: ©Joe M500

Velvet Lounge
photo: ©Josh Jackson

The Empty Bottle photo:
©The Empty Bottle

BEFORE YOU GO, GET IN THE KNOW

Websites:

www.umbrellamusic.org

www.jazzchicago.net

www.lib.uchicago.edu/e/su/cja

www.jazzinchicago.org

www.now-is.org

Publications:

The Chicago Reader

Chicago Jazz Magazine

Although jazz was born in and around New Orleans, there's little doubt that any other city was more responsible for its development and increasing popularity during the 1920s than Chicago. Boasting abundant employment opportunities, a rich culture, and the possibility for social advancement (including the chance to hold public office), Chicago came to be known as one of the most desirable and livable locations for African-Americans, who steadily migrated to the city's South Side throughout the decade.

As the population swelled, a vast network of nightclubs emerged, where legendary figures like Louis Armstrong, Jelly Roll Morton, King Oliver, and Earl "Fatha" Hines regularly performed and recorded. Much of the action shifted to New York as the 20s drew to a close, but Chicago remained a magnet for southern blacks. So, for the next two decades, jazz, along with blues and rhythm & blues,

> **Chicago Theater** photo:©Mike Warot

Earl "Fatha" Hines

A pianist who was one of many musicians attracted by Chicago's bustling scene in the 20s. He stuck around, setting up shop with an influential big band at the Grand Terrace Café, where he gave Charlie Parker one of his first pro gigs and where loose after-hours jam sessions laid the foundation for bebop.

Sun Ra (a.k.a Herman Blount)

He burst onto the Chicago scene in the mid-50s. His group spent its early years modernizing the sound of Fletcher Henderson's great orchestra. By the end of the decade, Ra had incorporated electric keyboards and started dressing his orchestra in wild costumes, planting the seeds of the 60s free-jazz explosion. photo: ©Tobias Akerboom

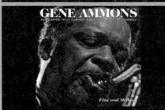

Gene Ammons

Got his start with Woody Herman's band, but made his mark in a two-tenor group with fellow DuSable vet Sonny Stitt. Ammons's melodic improvisations, imbued with a strong bluesiness and a breathy sensitivity derived from the great Ben Webster, were crowd-pleasers.

Von Freeman

Another DuSable alum and one of the more adventurous tenor players in Chicago. His sharp, biting tone remains a fixture on the scene today. Although he's a dyed-in-the-wool hard bopper, Freeman has never been afraid to take the music out; in fact, you could say he's more daring than his son, Chico Freeman. photo: ©Vincenzo Innocente

The Art Ensemble of Chicago

Led a small exodus of progressive Chicago musicians to Paris. Probably the best known and most eclectic product of the AACM, the band—trumpeter Lester Bowie, bassist Malachi Favors, drummer Don Moye, and reedists Joseph Jarman and Roscoe Mitchell—smashed all preconceptions of what a "jazz" group could accomplish, living up to the AACM motto, "Great Black Music - Ancient to the Future." photo: ©Paulo Borgia

Anthony Braxton

Polymath, reedist, and composer. A hero of the AACM, he is a fearless explorer who cut the first-ever album of solo saxophone performances. Never having felt the need to reconcile his love for cool jazz artists and avant-garde composers, Braxton has collaborated with everyone from Dave Brubeck to Wolf Eyes. photo: ©David Shechter

Fred Anderson

A big-toned tenor saxophonist involved in the genesis of the AACM. Even though he soon went his own way, he's had a huge impact on Chicago for more than four decades, taking musicians like George Lewis and Hamid Drake under his wing. photo: ©neonwar

Ken Vandermark

A reedist who put Chicago jazz back on the map in the 90s, sparking a free jazz and improvised-music explosion that shows no signs of abating. He searches out unconventional spaces in which to present his music, attracting a new audience by taking his high-energy free jazz into rock clubs rather than stuffy jazz venues. photo: ©Andy Newcombe

Rob Mazurek

A cornetist who started out as a hardline hard-bopper. After discovering the Art Ensemble of Chicago, he opened up his musical imagination and began a fruitful partnership with Tortoise guitarist Jeff Parker. They've released a series of thrilling albums under the moniker The Chicago Underground. photo: ©Angela Novaes

Nicole Mitchell

The current president of the AACM, and one of the greatest flute players on the planet. With her band Black Earth Ensemble, Mitchell has composed a series of extended suites drawing inspiration from figures like Alice Coltrane and Octavia Butler. photo: ©Michael Jackson

INFLUENTIAL CHICAGO JAZZ ALBUMS

Gene Ammons
The Gene Ammons Story: Gentle Jug (1961-63)

Sun Ra
Jazz in Silhouette (1958)

Anthony Braxton
3 Compositions of New Jazz (1968)

Von Freeman
The Improvisor (2002)

Nicole Mitchell's Black Earth Ensemble
Black Unstoppable (2007)

Louis Armstrong
The Complete Hot Five and Hot Seven Recordings (1925-28)

Earl "Fatha" Hines
Earl Hines and the Duke's Men (1944-47)

Art Ensemble of Chicago
Americans Swinging in Paris: The Pathe Sessions (1969-70)

Fred Anderson & Hamid Drake
From the River to the Ocean (2007)

Vandermark 5
Beat Reader (2008)

continued to thrive. Hard bop flourished in the 50s, engendered by tenor greats like Gene Ammons, Sonny Stitt, Johnny Griffin, John Gilmore, and Von Freeman, and the one-and-only Sun Ra, who began formulating his magical take on Afro-Futurist big band music.

Things changed in the 60s, when Chicago's economy started to collapse. Taverns opted for organ trios or DJs to cut costs, leaving most musicians hungry for work. Out of this atmosphere came the AACM (Association for the Advancement of Creative Musicians), a group of daring individuals who took matters into their own hands. They set up their own concert series, did their own promotion, and shredded the rules of jazz orthodoxy, freeing themselves to draw upon whatever traditions they saw fit. AACM greats like the Art Ensemble of Chicago, Muhal Richard Abrams, Leo Smith, Anthony Braxton, and Henry Threadgill—to name but a few—established Chicago as a hub for experimentation, and four decades later, their model still thrives.

Many of the AACM's leading lights ended up in New York by the mid-70s, leading to a somewhat fallow time in Chicago. But those who remained, including tenor great Fred Anderson and isolated

---

> [top] **Association for Advancement of Creative Musicians** photo: ©Steve Silverman
[bottom] **Art Ensemble of Chicago** photo: ©Paulo Borgia

ART IMITATING LIFE:
THE MUSIC IN MOVIES

Films About Artists:

Let's Get Lost (1988)
Director: Bruce Weber

Thelonious Monk: Straight, No Chaser (1988)
Director: Charlotte Zwerin

Bird (1988)
Director: Clint Eastwood

Young Man with a Horn (1950)
Director: Michael Curtiz

Space is the Place (1974)
Director: John Coney

Kansas City (1996)
Director: Robert Altman

Round Midnight (1986)
Director: Bertrand Tavernier

Soundtracks Featuring Artists' Music:

Shadows (1959)
Director: John Cassavetes

Blow-Up (1966)
Director: Michelangelo Antonioni

Elevator to the Gallows (1958)
Director: Louis Malle

Anatomy of a Murder (1959)
Director: Otto Preminger

Sweet Smell of Success (1957)
Director: Alexander Mackendrick

Naked Lunch (1991)
Director: David Cronenberg

> [top] **Chicago Cultural Center** photo:©Mike Warot
> [bottom] **Umbrella Festival** photo: ©Maureen Lin

SEE IT FOR YOURSELF

photo: ©karaian

Chicago Jazz Festival (Chicago)
The programming is diverse—and often a mixed bag in terms of quality—but the best thing about this behemoth festival, held every September in Grant Park, is that admission is free.

Umbrella Music Festival (Chicago)
While at heart a showcase for the city's more adventurous musicians, this annual event taking place in November typically includes a handful of national heavies and up to a half-dozen acts from Europe, brought in as part of an initiative with local branches of foreign consulates.

Edgefest (Ann Arbor, MI)
Held each October, this festival takes place at multiple venues, including the Kerrytown Concert House, and features progressive and avant-garde jazz.

Vision Festival (New York, NY)
Inspired by the 1981 and 1984 Sound Unity Festivals, this event showcases experimental music (predominantly avant-garde and free jazz), art, film, and dance. It is held on the Lower East Side every year in June.

Festival International de Musique Actuelle de Victoriaville (Victoriaville, Quebec)
This international music festival takes place every year in May and features contemporary jazz music.

mavericks like reedist-drummer Hal Russell, kept things cooking. The scene exploded again in the mid-90s, and at the center of it all was reedist Ken Vandermark, who combined the ideals of the AACM and the brash energy of Russell with strong European influences. The fervor of his music attracted a new, younger audience. Before too long, thanks in part to the emergence of the so-called post-rock scene—spearheaded by like-minded, forward-looking groups like Tortoise and Gastr del Sol—musicians started flocking to the city. Eventually Vandermark and music journalist John Corbett started a weekly series at The Empty Bottle (a rock club) and things sprouted from there. Spaces have come and gone, but there hasn't been a serious drought in 15 years. Now the scene is stronger and more diverse than ever, with the musician-run Umbrella Music Collective driving much of the action.

⌃ **The Hideout (Shotgun Party)**
photo: ©Matthew Ginger
⟩ **The Empty Bottle** photo: ©Liz Bustamante

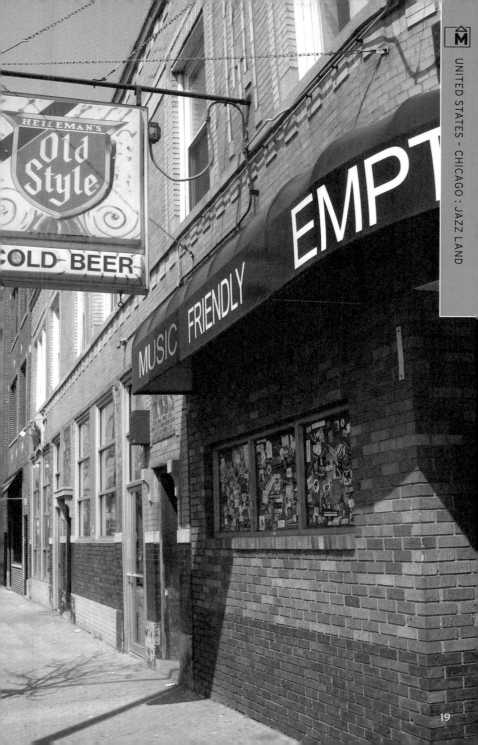

Chicago Bean Panorama photo ©Mike Warot

MAP OF VENUES
AND CITY LANDMARKS

1 Jazz Showcase
Hosts a who's who of national acts, from vets like James Moody to new bloods such as Kurt Rosenwinkel.
806 S. Plymouth Ct.
+ 312 360 0234

2 Velvet Lounge
Presents adventurous jazz. The most reliable place to catch old and new members of the AACM.
67 E. Cermak Rd.
+ 312 791 9050

3 New Apartment Lounge
The amoeba-shaped Formica bar is certainly worth a gander, plus Von Freeman leads his jam session here every Tuesday night.
504 E. 75th St.
+ 773 483 7728

4 Green Mill
With the exception of the Cultural Center, this is the only extant venue in Chicago that could qualify as a genuine landmark.
4802 N. Broadway
+ 773 878 5552

5 Hideout
One of the friendliest and warmest music venues in town. Also plays host to the Umbrella Music Festival.
1354 W. Wabansia Ave.
+ 773 227 4433

6 Hungry Brain
Most nights it's jukebox music, but that changes on Sundays, when Umbrella Music presents their "Sunday Transmission" series, a dynamic mix of local and touring acts. Their annual festival takes place here too.

2319 W. Belmont Ave.
+ 773 935 2118

7 Chicago Cultural Center
One of the city's greatest treasures, a true palace of culture where everything is free: concerts, film screenings, art exhibitions, dance performances, and more.
78 E. Washington St.
+ 312 744 6630

8 Elastic
An unassuming, comfortable, non-profit space that programs a wide range of adventurous music, particularly of the jazz and free-improvised variety. This space also plays host to the Umbrella Music Festival.
2830 N. Milwaukee Ave.
+ 773 772 3616

9 Jazz Record Mart
One of the oldest, largest, and greatest jazz and blues record shops in the world.
27 E. Illinois St.
+ 312 222 1467

10 Empty Bottle
A well-known rock club where Ken Vandermark and music journalist John Corbett started their weekly series.
1035 N. Western Ave.
+ 773 276 3600

11 Dusty Groove
Features an excellent, carefully curated mix of CDs and LPs (the used vinyl includes many rarities) with an emphasis on jazz, soul, and Brazilian music.
1120 N. Ashland Ave.
+ 773 342 5800

Edison P

HARWOOD
HEIGHTS

90

W Belmont Av

W Fullerton Av

ELMWOOD
PARK

W North Av

rk

BERWYN

43

5

Bedford
Park

UPTOWN

North Park

W Lawrence Ave 4

Albany Park

RAVENSWOOD

94

WRIGLEYVILLE

AVONDA 6 ROSCOE
VILLAGE

8

BUCKTOWN

Humboldt
Park 5

OAK
PARK

WEST TOWN 10 11

East Garfield GOOSE
Park ISLAND

N Lake Shore Dr

NEAR
NORTH SIDE

9

90 7

W Randolph St

CHICAGO

Kennedy Expy

1 41

290

Eisenhower Expy

94

CICERO 2 NEAR
SOUTH SIDE

W Cermak Rd

55

Adlai E Stevenson Expy

McKINLEY
PARK

90

Gage Park

S Lake Shore Dr

41
Hyde Park

Dan Ryan Expy

OAK LAWN ENGLEWOOD

Chicago Skyway

50

3

AVALON PARK 23

02: BRING THE NOISE, BRING THE PUNK

by James Hendicott

18th c. ▶▶

Penny whistles, throbbing fiddles, and banjos come to Dublin via farm laborers.

1950s ▶▶

Irish folk music becomes an international trend.

1970s–1990s ▶▶

Irish immigration foments Celtic punk in expatriate strongholds, London and New York.

2000s

Approximately 92% of people of Irish descent live outside the Republic, making the dissemination of Dublin-style punk a natural progression.

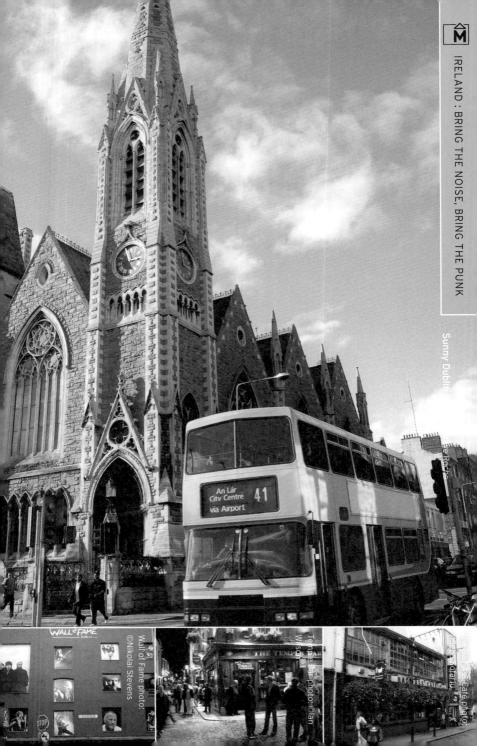

Sunny Dublin

An Lár
City Centre **41**
via Airport

WALL of FAME

@Nikolai Stevens

Wall of Fame photo:

Temple Bar photo:@Ian
Wilson

If you only see one band in Dublin, make it Blood or Whiskey. They mix harmonicas and tin whistles with all the raw aggression of modern-day punk rock, and they embody the spirit of the Celtic punk scene, where at sweat-drenched shows in dingy basements, headbangers throw back pints of Guinness with shamrocks peeking through swirls of foam. Men with Mohawks and piercings bounce around joyfully as bands thrash away at unfathomable speed, brimming with national pride.

Too fun to be angry and too raw to be fashionable, this vibrant scene could only be in Ireland's capital, where the world's most famous pubs provide the backdrop, and the stars are the freshly brewed pints of "the black stuff," the playful dancing, and the loud, lairy, all-night-long music. Ireland's rural traditions—combined with hundreds of years of defying English occupation—inform Dublin's boisterous music scene, which stretches from superclub warehouses to tiny cafés populated by one man and his guitar to the underground roar of Celtic punk.

BEFORE YOU GO, GET IN THE KNOW

Websites:

www.state.ie
www.paddyrock.com
www.shitenonions.com
www.bloodorwhiskey.ie

Books:

The Philosophy of Punk: More than Noise
by Craig O'Hara

Thin Lizzy
by Alan Byrne

Rock n' Stroll: Dublin's Music Trail
by Dublin Tourism

Irish Folk, Trad and Blues
by Colin Harper

Green Suede Shoes
by Larry Kirwan

Pogue Mahone Kiss My Arse: The Story of the Pogues
by Carol Clerk

^ [top] **The streets of Temple Bar district** photo: ©Fhwrdh
[middle] **The Abbey Tavern in Howth** photo: ©John Picken
[bottom] **Eamonn Doran** photo: ©Shadowgate

27

HOMETOWN HEROES

Phil Lynott
The legendary singer, bassist, songwriter and front man for Thin Lizzy. His statue in Temple Bar is a spot revered by local street musicians (and often fought over). photo: ©RinzeWind

Blood or Whiskey
Ireland's current-day Celtic punk heroes. They've fought through a member's death, jail time, and numerous lineup changes.
photo: ©Pat O'Leary

The Dubliners
Formed in 1962, the Irish folk band that started it all. They made a name for themselves by playing regular gigs at O'Donoghue's Pub.
photo: ©Henry Schmidt

Paranoid Visions
Formed in 1982, this infamous punk band from Dublin broke up 10 years later, but recently decided to give it another go with the release of a new album in January 2009.
photo: ©Stuart Chalmers

Spud N*ggers (a.k.a Da Spuds)
The controversial Celt rockers from Athlone. The name of the band comes from a less-than-PC reference to the Irish niche in the old-world caste system famously paraphrased in the film *The Commitments*.
photo: ©Kimberly Lightholder

Horslips
Formed in 1970, the Horslips were one of the original Celtic rock bands. They composed, arranged, and performed their songs based on traditional Irish jigs and reels. They called it quits in 1980, but in 2005 the original line-up reunited and performed a few shows.
photo: ©Daragh Owens

The Undertones
Ireland's answer to the Sex Pistols. Formed in 1976 and hailing from Derry, this band released four albums before breaking up in 1983.
photo: ©Alterna2

Bob Geldof
The Irish singer, songwriter, actor and political activist who entered the public conscience originally as a member of the rock band The Boomtown Rats.
photo: ©Erik Charlton

ALBUMS THAT INFLUENCED CELTIC PUNK ROCK IN DUBLIN

The Dubliners
Seven Drunken Nights (1967)

Thin Lizzy
Jailbreak (1976)

The Skids
Scared to Dance (1979)

The Pogues
Rum, Sodomy & the Lash (1985)

Blood or Whiskey
Self-Titled (1996)

The Pogues
If I Should Fall from Grace with God (1987)

The Dropkick Murphys
Sing Loud, Sing Proud (2001)

Flogging Molly
Drunken Lullabies (2002)

Blood or Whiskey
Cashed out on Culture (2005)

Paranoid Visions
40 Shades of Gangreen (2007)

Like punk rock itself, Celtic punk is a rebellion-fueled aural barrage. Combining traditional Irish instrumentation with electric guitars and other "rock" sounds, it could be described as Irish folk played hard and in a serious hurry. While Celtic Punk may sound upbeat and lighthearted, especially compared to the stereotypical grimness of British punk, its sunny swagger and wild abandon just give a different face to the same potent energy. Irish musicians play angry rebel songs with wry smiles on their faces, and they play them almost anywhere.

The roots of Celtic punk date back to 18th-century agricultural Ireland, where—as a break from lamenting British imperialism—folk music helped pass the drizzly winters. Much of this was first performed by solo singers, but by the time it drifted to Dublin, piercing penny whistles, staccato fiddles, and twanging banjos had been added to the heartfelt vocals. At its peak in the late 1950s, Irish folk music was an international success, and more orchestral acts like The Dubliners and The Chieftains created a spin-off genre, Celtic fusion.

Famine, war, and economics have long led the Irish to travel—often within the bosom of their Imperial

neighbor—and it was amongst expats that Celtic punk took shape. In the 70s and 80s, émigrés gathered in London's Irish bars, celebrating their heritage with traditional music nights. Around the same time, of course, punk rock was being imported across the pond from New York City. Acts like The Pogues (a London-based group with Irish heritage) and The Skids (based in Fife, Scotland) were the first to combine the propulsive drumming and rich melodic clatter of Celtic folk with the full-on electric assault of punk. The Pogues, in particular, made a big impact: it didn't take long for their sound, essentially the template for Celtic punk, to return to its spiritual home.

Since then, Celtic punk has gradually wiggled its way into the heart of the Irish pub scene, as well as gained international notoriety through American acts like Dropkick Murphys and Flogging Molly, who have sold over two million albums between them. Even Germany (with Fiddler's Green) and South Korea (with St. John the Gambler) have their own stars.

Hunting down Dublin's own Celtic punk isn't as easy as it sounds, but make the effort and you'll be rewarded. The cobbled streets of Temple Bar are a great place to start, with nightly performances of anything and everything with an Irish twang drifting from each old oak door. Traditional folk bars like O'Donoghue's (the legendary hangout of The Dubliners, which feels like the inside of a large tree) and The Abbey Tavern in Howth offer more mellow sounds and traditional Irish ambience, and the famous Grafton Street buskers

ʌ [top] **Buskers in Temple Bar** photo: ©Fhwrdh
[bottom] **Dropkick Murphys** photo: ©Chris Friese

Riverside buildings in Dublin photo: ©Thierry Malfeis

provide an eclectic wall of sounds by which to peruse the shops. These unsung heroes—musicians who turn up every week to rock a host of city center bars with their own brand of shamrock culture, á la 2007's *Once*—are perhaps the most memorable musical features of this ancient city. But to find some authentic, all-Irish Celtic punk, you may need an invite to one of those sweat-drenched basements.

Ireland's acceptance of Celtic punk has been cautious, though such hybrids actually go pretty far back on the Emerald Isle. From Thin Lizzy's rampaging cover of "Whiskey in the Jar" to Black 47's "Funky Céilí," rock has formed easy matches with traditional Irish forms for decades. The contribution of Irish folk music to good old American rock 'n' roll, by way of Appalachian folk, could well have helped the matchmaking process. Of course, there's been no shortage of straight-up Irish rock bands, from Thin Lizzy and The Undertones to That Petrol Emotion, and of course, U2.

Surprisingly, Dublin's initial reaction to iconic rockers and Irish natives Blood or Whiskey was a hostile one. Their musical blend was close enough to old Irish folk for traditionalists to describe it as sacrilegious, an impression their booze-soaked, obscenity-ridden lyrics did nothing to dispel, but Blood or Whiskey soldiered on, eventually winning over many locals. They certainly don't have the luck of the Irish (or do they?), but the six-piece continues to defy detractors with their punked-up Celtic pride.

Plenty of other local artists are getting in on the act, too. Athlone's provocatively named Spud N*ggers (a.k.a. Da Spuds) offer a punk-rock infused Celtic riot. Though less overt in hardcore Dublin bands Paranoid Visions and Red Army, a definite Celtic tinge has edged into the city's heavier music over the past decade.

With around 70 of 76 million people of Irish descent living outside the Republic, it's no surprise that Celtic punk has developed in large part away from Ireland, but Dublin is where it comes together with Irish folk music and all its rocked-up derivatives.

^ **Frontman Father Jack from Da Spuds** photo: ©Kimberly Lightholder
< [top] **O'Connell Street General Post Office located next to The Spire of Dublin, a landmark built in the south of the city to celebrate the new millennium** photo: ©Dublin Tourism
[bottom] **Blood or Whiskey** photo: ©Pat O' Leary

SEE IT
FOR YOURSELF

Guinness Irish Festival
(Sion, Switzerland)
An annual festival that features a variety of Irish music. Usually held in August.

Temple Bar TradFest
(Dublin)
A festival of Irish music of all kinds. Held annually in late January/early February.

photo: ©TASCQ Industry partner of Dublin Tourism

Reading Festival
(Reading, England)
An all-round heavy music festival that invariably features a small selection of heavy Celtic Punk bands. It's held every year in late August.

photo: ©Mark Freeman

Saturday night's inevitable barrage of Irish-themed cover songs are impossible to miss, but even in watching the local pub's regulars stretch their vocal chords after a liquid lunch, you simply can't avoid soaking in the cacophony of new and old.

From that spot under the statue of Thin Lizzy's Phil Lynott, fought over by street musicians due to its iconic status, to Bewley's, the pub where Bob Geldof and his Boomtown Rats knocked together their debut album, Dublin has music in its soul. So much so that native son Elvis Costello once told an interviewer that "when picked apart, all music goes back to Scotland or Ireland." He may have been exaggerating, but on a night out in Dublin, it doesn't feel like it.

^ **Streets of Dublin** photo: ©Seba Sofariu
› **Traditional pub in Temple Bar**
photo: ©Jo Jakeman

MAP OF VENUES
AND CITY LANDMARKS

1 Wall Of Fame/Temple Bar
The musical landmark of Ireland's hometown heroes.
Rockarchive Gallery
U3, 20 Temple Lane South
+ 633 4146

2 The Phil Lynott Statue
The iron likeness of Thin Lizzy's famous frontman.
Harry St.

3 Bad Ass Cafe
The old workplace of Irish rocker Sinead O'Connor.
9/11 Crown Alley
+ 671 2596

4 Claddagh Records
A record shop and label known for innovation and originality.
24 Dame St.
+ 679 3664

5 Celtic Note Music Store
The place to buy all things Irish music.
14/15 Nassau St.
+ 670 4157

6 Temple Bar
Dublin's music district. Extends from Fishamble Street in the west to Westmoreland Street in the east, and from the River Liffey in the north to Lord Edward Street-Dame Street-College Green in the south.

7 Bewley's
An old Grafton Street haunt of hometown hero Bob Geldof.
2 Grafton St.
+ 672 7720

8 Road Records
A record store specializing in Irish independent music.
16B Fade St.
+ 671 7340

9 O'Donoghue's
The legendary hangout of hometown heroes, The Dubliners.
15 Merrion Row
+ 660 7194

10 The Academy
A popular alternative music venue.
57 Middle Abbey St.
+ 877 9999

11 The Baggot Inn
An energetic, live music pub.
143 Lower Baggot St.
+ 661 8758

12 Whelan's
An iconic live pub and two-stage venue.
25 Wexford St.
+ 478 0766

13 The Cobblestone
A well-known traditional Irish music pub.
77 King St. North
+ 872 1799

14 Eamonn Doran
A popular alternative music bar.
3A Crown Alley
+ 679 9114

15 Abbey Tavern
Traditional out-of-town bar and music venue.
28 Abbey St., Howth
+ 839 0307

Little Britain St

Mary's Ln

O'connell St

Talbot St

Middle Abbey St

10

Eden Quay

Swift's Row

N11

Burgh Quay

Tara Street

Ormond Quay

Aston Quay

Tara St

Essex Quay

Wettington Quay

3 **1**

14

Dame St

4 **6** **N81**

Grafton St

Pearse St

N81

DUBLIN

7

Nicholas St

S Great Georges St

Drury St

8

Chatham Ln

2

N11

Nassau St

5

Dawson St

Clare St

Kildare St

Merrion Square N

Merrion Square Park

Aungier St

N11

St. Stephen's Green

Upper Merrion St

9

Lower Baggot St

Cuffe St

St Stephen's Green

St Stephen's Green

11

Camden Row **12**

Lower Camden St

Harcourt St

Howth Rd **R105**

Greenfield Rd

15

R105

Thornanby Rd

R105

39

03: NEW RAP CITY

by Miles Marshall Lewis

1980s ▶▶

Hip-hop is imported to France from New York City after President Mitterrand loosens state controls on radio airwaves, which allows private stations to get licensed and air international music.

1990 ▶▶

Rapattitude, a compilation album of homegrown French MCs and hip-hop, is a mainstream success and creates a commercially viable genre.

1993 ▶▶

Seminal rap group IAM releases *Ombre et Lumière*, with Islam and Northern Africa prominently mentioned, fostering a fanbase of young French-Arabs.

2005

Several weeks of nonstop rioting in Parisian suburbs during the last days of Ramadan, after two Muslim teenagers die in a police-related confrontation.

Le Havre
Paris
Boulogne-Billancourt
Issy-les-Moulineaux
Plan-de-Cuques
Marseille

Pont Alexandre III Bridge and the dome of the Invalides at night, Paris. photo: ©Erick Nguyen

October 27 2005. One year after the riots began, Paris. photo: ©PS Olivier sous-Bois City.

Arc de Triomphe photo: ©Serge Melki

Elysée Montmartre photo: ©Maxim Doucet

ELYSEE
MONTMARTRE

Entering the veiled world of Muslim hip-hop in Paris requires a certain amount of time travel.

First rewind the clock back to October 2005 and the notorious weeks of rioting that had Parisian suburbs in flames, and then turn it back even further, to the origins of French hip-hop culture itself, in the early 1980s. You'll soon see that Muslim hip-hop isn't really as distinct a genre as, say, Christian rock music, and that if you throw a stone into the pool of modern French rap, the ripples are bound to strike some Islamic beats and rhymes.

The spotlight was turned on the French Muslim population (between four to six million strong, the largest in Western Europe) in the last days of Ramadan 2005. The banlieues—or outlying suburbs—of Paris went wild for nearly three weeks after two Muslim teenagers were killed in a police-related confrontation. Ziad Benna, Bouana Traoré, and Muhttin Altun ran into an electric plant in Clichy-sous-Bois to hide from the local police, who had chased the teenagers down when they refused to show their IDs. Benna and

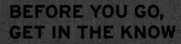

BEFORE YOU GO, GET IN THE KNOW

Websites:

www.cafedelasoul.com

www.furthermucker.com

Books:

Black France
by Dominic Thomas
(Parsels Prupre [1989] reproduced by kind permission of Cheri Samba)

Sufi Rapper
by Abd al Malik
(www.InnerTraditions.com)

Black, Blanc, Beur
edited by Alain-Philippe Durand

Rendezvous Eighteenth
by Jake Lamar

The Color of Liberty
edited by Sue Peabody and
Tyler Stovall

Paris Noir
by Tyler Stovall

Paris Reflections
by Christiann Anderson and
Monique Y. Wells

Harlem in Montmartre
by William A. Shack

Soul on the Seine
by Robin Nicole Bates

^ [top] **Paris, France** photo: ©Fddi1
[bottom] **L'Institut Du Monde Arabe** photo: ©Daquella Manera

HOMETOWN HEROES

Akhenaton With French-Italian roots, this artist hails from Marseille and was a founding member of IAM. He later released four solo albums and is known as a major figure in Muslim hip-hop today.
photo: ©Francis Bourgouin

Keny Arkana Originally from Argentina but hailing from Boulogne-Billancourt, Keny has released two albums and three EPs. She's also very active with the music collective La Rage Du Peuple.
photo: ©Jonas Roux

Médine Hailing from Le Havre, this French-Algerian rapper has been part of the hip-hop collective La Boussole and has been distributed through Din Records since 1996.

Fabe Hailing from Garges-les-Gonnesses with origins in Martinique, this French rapper released four successful albums before calling it quits to devote himself entirely to practicing his faith.

Abd al Malik This French-Congolese rapper and spoken word artist has released three albums and one book titled *Sufi Rapper*.
photo: ©Simon Robic

Ali Hailing from Issy-les-Moulineaux and of Moroccan descent, this former member of Lunatic has released six albums and found great success as a solo artist.

ART IMITATING LIFE:
THE MUSIC IN MOVIES

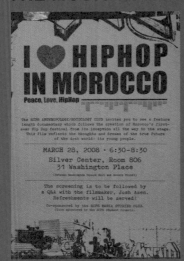

photo: ©katchua

I Love Hip-Hop in Morocco (2007)
Directors: Joshua Asen and
Jennifer Needleman

Slingshot Hip-Hop (2008)
Director: Jackie Reem Salloum

La Haine (The Hate) (1995)
Directed: Mathieu Kassovitz

Mr. Devious (2006)
Director: John Fredericks

Wild Style (1983)
Director: Charlie Ahearn

New Muslim Cool (2009)
Director: Jennifer Maytorena Taylor

Fangafrika (2008)
Directors: StayCalm! Productions and
West African Hip Hop

Ma 6-T Va Crack-er (My City Is Going To Crack) (1997)
Director: Jean-François Richet

Life of Jesus (1998)
Director: Bruno Dumont

Deen Tight (2009)
Director: Mustafa Davis

ALBUMS THAT INFLUENCED MUSLIM HIP-HOP IN PARIS

IAM
L'École du Micro d'Argent (The School of the Silver Mic) (1997)

Akhenaton
Métèque et Mat (Checkmate) (1999)

Keny Arkana
Entre Ciment et Belle Étoile (Between Cement and Beautiful Stars) (2006)

MBS
Le Micro Brise le Silence (The Mic Breaks the Silence) (2000)

Sinik
Sang Froid (Cold Blood) (2006)

Médine
11 Septembre, Récit du 11ème Jour (September 11, or the Narrative of the Same Day) (2004)

Abd al Malik
Le Face à Face des Cœurs (Hearts Face to Face) (2004)

Fabe
Befa Surprend Ses Frères (Befa Surprises His Brothers) (1996)

Ali
Chaos et Harmonie (Chaos and Harmony) (2005)

Various Artists
Morts Pour Rien (Dead for Nothing) (2007)

Traoré accidentally electrocuted themselves, and their deaths blew the lid off the pressure cooker of the cités (housing projects mostly located in the Parisian suburbs, unlike their inner-city American counterparts). Thousands of cars were torched in protest, close to 3,000 rioters were arrested, and President Jacques Chirac declared a national state of emergency.

Muslim hip-hop commemorated the tragedy several months later with *Morts Pour Rien (Dead for Nothing)*, a compilation album put together by rapper Kery James to benefit the dead teens' families. Featuring proudly Islamic MCs like Akhenaton and Sefyu, *Morts Pour Rein* detailed ethnic French discrimination and the invisibility

of Muslims of color in France. The reporterly detail of the MCs' rhymes is worth the listen even without the frenetic production. Public Enemy's Chuck D once famously called rap music "CNN for black people," and in France, Muslim hip-hop gives listeners an inside view of the marginalized lives of the Islamic French.

Hip-hop culture famously originated back in the late 70s and the South Bronx (NYC) community center jams of DJs Kool Herc, Afrika Bambaataa, and Grandmaster Flash. But France didn't get a true taste of rap music until President François Mitterrand loosened state control of the radio airwaves in 1981, licensing new, privately controlled radio stations; a few of these specialized in overseas hip-hop. DJ Dee Nasty, a disc jockey for Radio Nova, put out *Panam City Rappin'* (the first French rap album) in 1984. That same year, channel TF1 put "H.I.P. H.O.P." on the air, creating a TV outlet for the B-boying (or breakdancing) movement that was sweeping through Paris.

But rap in France didn't break the mainstream until the 1990 release of *Rapattitude,* a compilation album full

---

^ [top] **An image from the march held one year after the riots in Clichy-sous-Bois. The sign reads: "Bouna/Zied. Dead for Nothing."** photo: ©PS Clichy-sous-Bois
[bottom] **Album cover of 1990's** *Rapattitude*

of MCs who finally made homegrown hip-hop seem as viable as the American variety. In the wake of *Rapattitude* came the first real wave of iconic French rappers: Suprême NTM, Ministère AMER, and IAM. At the center of this trio of groups was Akhenaton of IAM, perhaps the best-known Muslim rapper in France.

Born Philippe Fragione in Marseilles, Akhenaton grew up in the small town of Plan-de-Cuques, raised by Italian parents who'd emigrated to France before he was born. He began to MC as a teenager in B.Boys Stance, renamed IAM in 1989. Two-thirds of the six-member group chose ancient Egyptian MC names: Shurik'n, Khéops, Imhotep and Akhenaton himself, signaling their solidarity with their largely Arab fanbase and championing reconnection with their North African culture.

A socially conscious group like Public Enemy or Boogie Down Productions, IAM was responsible for the seminal albums *IAM Concept* (1990) and *Ombre est Lumière* (1993). Islam was always central to the group's image and lyrics. Akhenaton went solo in 1995, releasing *Métèque et Mat* (an album with obvious Islamic overtones) and three more albums since, but still collaborates with IAM, using Arab-Islamic lyrics in an attempt to increase tolerance for Muslims through familiarity.

Yet Muslim hip-hop isn't a monolithic force in Paris, even in the Arab-French community. There are Muslim MCs in France who don't wear their spiritual beliefs like a badge of honor. Booba, a high-profile French-Senegalese rapper from Boulogne-Billancourt, is embroiled in an American-style rap feud with French-Algerian rapper Sinik. Booba is Muslim, but in the gangsta MC mold, he's not overly concerned with walking the righteous path. Suffice it to say, for every Muslim-and-proud MC like the French-Congolese rap artist Abd al Malik, there's another rapper of Islamic faith rocking microphones without mentioning Allah at all.

The scene could be compared to the U.S., where MCs in the African-American Nation of Islam might be discreet about their membership (Snoop Dogg) or blatant (Ice Cube). Islamic hip-hop in the U.S. gained its greatest following during rap's "consciousness" era (1987–1991). MCs following the precepts of the Nation of Gods and Earths (a.k.a. the Five Percent Nation, a more radical offshoot of the Nation of Islam) were plentiful: Brand Nubian, Rakim, Poor Righteous Teachers, and Big Daddy Kane. Though Akhenaton has gone on record dissing these

< **IAM (Akhenaton) + Muzion 21/21** photo: ©Francis Bourgouin

A Notre Dame gargoyle overlooks Paris, photo ©Brian Jeffery Beggerly

black Americans as untrue to the pure Islamic faith, the influence of Five Percenters in hip-hop (and Muslim hip-hop particularly) can't be denied. Their influence can be found in everything from Wu-Tang Clan to current-day French star Keny Arkana.

Just as some say legendary Californian act N.W.A foreshadowed the riots that followed the Rodney King beating in their volatile rhymes, it's possible to credit French Muslim hip-hoppers like Sniper for warning of the immigrant powder keg that exploded into the 2005 banlieue riots. For this reason alone, Muslim hip-hop is worth the listen: to get an accurate picture of what's really happening in Paris, beyond the bright lights of the Seine and Champs-Élysées.

^ **Élysée Montmartre** photo: ©Emmanuel Digiaro
> **Mosque in Paris** photo: ©Lev Dolgachov

MAP OF VENUES AND CITY LANDMARKS

1 T Maxx Records
A few steps from the Place du Châtelet. A pure selection of albums and singles of funk and soul, but mostly devoted to hip-hop and R&B.
111 Rue St. Denis
+ 4233 3487

2 Crocodisc
Open since 1978. Specializes in buying and selling new discs, and offers all types of music except classical.
40 Rue des Écoles
+ 4354 3322

3 Monster Melodies
Secondhand shop that offers more than 10,000 CDs of every variety.
9 Rue des Déchargeurs
+ 4028 0939

photo: ©Jac Currie

4 Moby Disques
A small shop specializing in jazz and unique imports.
9 Rue Boucry
+ 4329 7051

5 Jussieu Music
Opened in 1989. A leading place to buy, sell, or exchange used CDs and DVDs. Has a large and rapidly changing selection.
20 Rue Linné
+ 4331 1418

6 Élysée Montmartre
One of Paris's most famous music venues with a capacity of 1200 people. Hosts bands of various genres from all over the globe.
72 Boulevard de Rochechouart
+ 4492 4536

7 La Boule Noire
A cozy venue. Great for checking out acts from out of town.
118 Boulevard de Rochechouart
+ 4925 8175

8 La Cigale
One of Paris's finest venues. Features a horseshoe-shaped theatre.
120 Boulevard de Rochechouart
+ 4925 8175

9 L' Olympia
Some of the biggest legends in music have performed here in the past (The Beatles, Hendrix). Albums have been recorded here, too. Contemporary acts of all genres hit the stage nowadays.
28 Boulevard des Capucines
+ 9268 3368

CLICHY

ET

Parc de Monceau

Bd Haussman

Cours La Rein

Quai d'C

Parc du Champs de Mars

R Leco

R de Vaugi

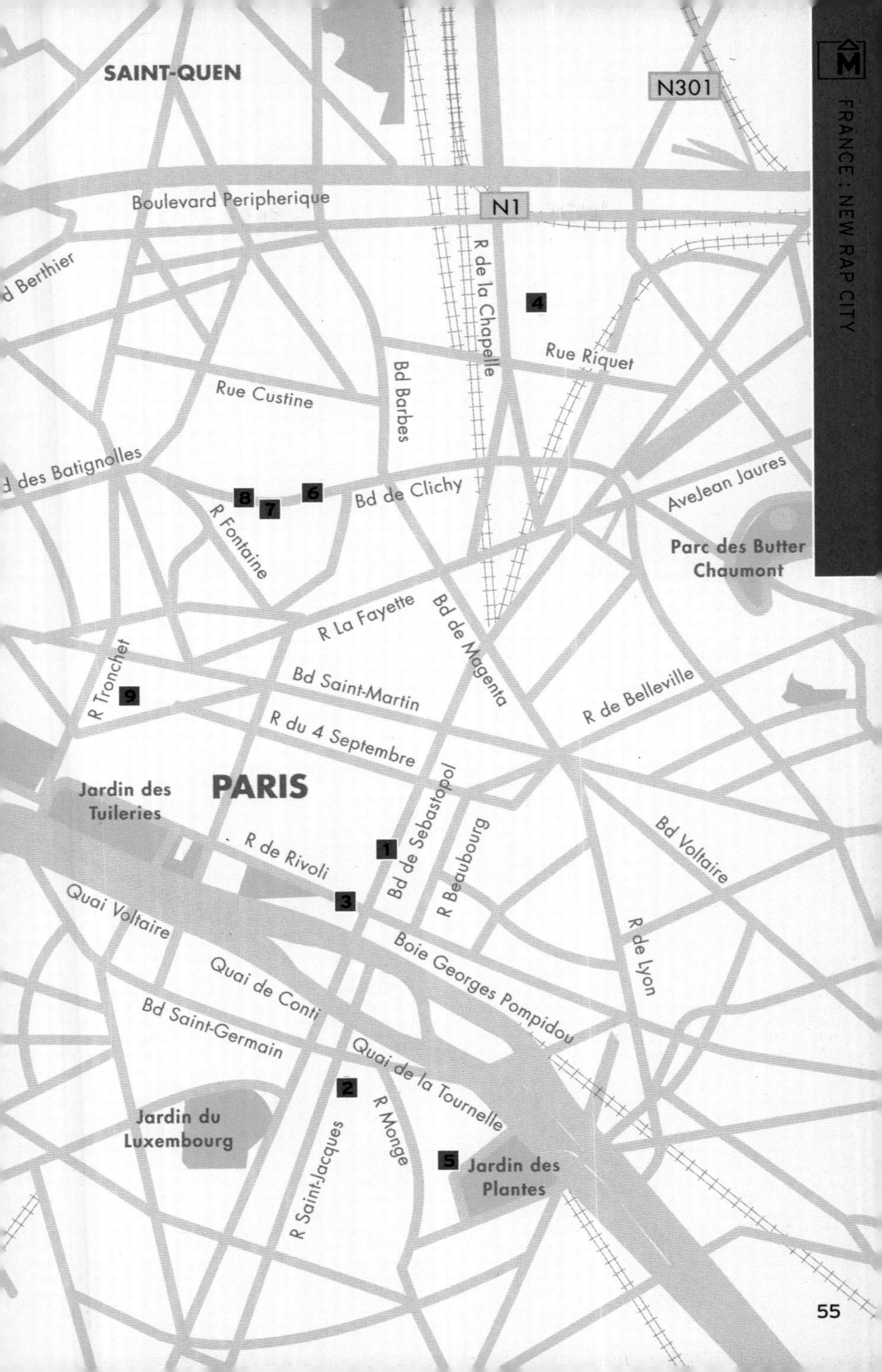

SAINT-QUEN

N301

Boulevard Peripherique

N1

d Berthier

R de la Chapelle

4

Rue Custine

Rue Riquet

Bd Barbes

d des Batignolles

8 **7** **6**

Bd de Clichy

AveJean Jaures

R Fontaine

Parc des Butter Chaumont

R La Fayette

Bd de Magenta

R Tronchet

9

Bd Saint-Martin

R de Belleville

R du 4 Septembre

Jardin des Tuileries

PARIS

R de Rivoli

Bd de Sebastopol

R Beaubourg

Bd Voltaire

1

3

Quai Voltaire

R de Lyon

Boie Georges Pompidou

Quai de Conti

Bd Saint-Germain

Quai de la Tournelle

2

R Monge

Jardin du Luxembourg

R Saint-Jacques

5

Jardin des Plantes

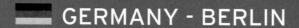

04: TECHNO COLOR

by Siobhan O'Leary

1970s ▶▶

Berlin and Detroit jointly birth the musical beginnings of techno through the experimental music of Kraftwerk as well as the disco of Donna Summer and Giorgio Moroder.

1989 ▶▶

Fall of the Berlin Wall. Techno explodes when the first Love Parade Festival occurs. It becomes an annual pilgrimage-making event for the next 20 years.

1991 ▶▶

Epicenter of commercial techno, Club Tresor, opens doors in what was East Berlin. The enterprise also spawns a record label.

2007

Club Tresor closes when the land it was on is sold to a developer. After a two-year reprieve, it reopens in a renovated power plant in Mitte.

Berlin ●

● Frankfurt

Berlin city photo:©Henry Sivonen

Berlin Cathedral photo:©Andrew Mason

Berlin Flaiga Clione. photo. ©Boliston

White Trash ©Tiloe

I ♡ Trash

BEFORE YOU GO, GET IN THE KNOW

Websites:

www.di.fm
www.ilovetechno.be
www.beatportal.com

Magazines:

www.raveline.de

Books:

Russian Disco by Wladimir Kaminer

Techno Rebels: The Renegades of Electronic Funk by Dan Sicko

Lost and Sound by Tobias Rapp

Last Night a DJ Saved My Life: The History of the Disc Jockey by Bill Brewster

Twenty years ago the Berlin Wall came tumbling down, and in the sound of the pounding jackhammers, you could hear the beat that would become the pulse of a generation. The story of German techno is of countless DJs who made their way to Berlin to hone their craft, and of a city that has survived a staggering amount of change, never losing its creative edge.

The origins of techno lie in the 70s, in the experimental music of Kraftwerk and the disco of Donna Summer and Giorgio Moroder. Detroit (Michigan), with its hometown heroes like Derrick May, was, in fact, the birthplace-proper of the form. But the music and movement only reached international proportions in the late 80s and early 90s with the emergence of Berlin's Love Parade. The first Love Parade, presided over by Dr. Motte and Westbam, was celebrated in 1989, four months before the fall of the Wall, when the time was ripe for political change. The Love

> [top] **Brandenburg Gate**
> photo: ©Wolfgang Staudt
> [bottom left] **Fall of the Berlin Wall 1989**
> photo: ©Gavinandrewstewart
> [bottom right] **The Love Parade**
> photo: ©Karsten Suehring

HOMETOWN HEROES

Henrik Schwarz
A Berlin-based icon known for fusing techno with other genres. Schwarz hails from the south of Germany and built his reputation in the early 1990s as someone who could mix techno and house with jazz and improvisation.
photo: ©Henrik Schwarz

Richie Hawtin
Grew up just across the border from Detroit, the birthplace of techno. By the age of 17, Hawtin was already mixing house and techno with a European influence. In 2003, he moved to Berlin, where he still spins in the top techno hotspots. photo: ©Pinkpucca

Ellen Allien
A native of Berlin, she has emerged as a huge techno pop star and is the most prominent woman in a primarily male-dominated scene. She got involved with music in London during the acid house revolution sparked by the Wag Club in 1988.
photo: ©zero.eu

Wladimir Kaminer

An icon of Berlin nightlife, thanks to his bi-monthly Russian Disco parties at his own Kaffee Burger. Kaminer emigrated from Moscow to Berlin more than a decade ago and found a city full of artists and drifters, who seemed idealist even in the face of destruction and poverty. photo: ©Andre Zehetbauer

Ricardo Villalobos

Born in Santiago, Chile, raised in Germany after his family fled there for political reasons when he was only three years old. Inspired by Depeche Mode and Plastikman, along with Brazilian music, he started DJing in the 1990s with a distinct mix of Latin and Detroit percussion and rhythm. photo: ©Lars Borges

Modeselektor

An electronic music band that formed in Berlin in 1992, and toured internationally, producing music with self-developed software. The band has collaborated with everyone from Thom Yorke to French rappers TTC. photo: ©Modeselektor

ALBUMS THAT INFLUENCED TECHNO IN BERLIN

Henrik Schwarz
Henrik Schwarz Live
(2007)

Kraftwerk
Computer World (1981)

Ellen Allien
Berlinette (2003)

Ricardo Villalobos
Fabric 36 (2007)

Modeselektor
Happy Birthday! (2007)

Gui Boratto
Chromophobia (2007)

Booka Shade
Movements (2006)

Essendon Airport
Sonic Investigations of the Trivial (2002)
Richie Hawtin
DE9: Closer to the Edit (2001)
Various Artists
Tresor Mix, Vol. 1-5 (2007-2008)
Derrick Carter & Mark Farina
Live at OM (2004)

Parade grew into an annual event on the Straße des 17. Juni in Berlin's Tiergarten. It featured the world's hottest techno DJs and drew crowds of over a million, some dressed in outlandish costumes and others wearing nothing at all. Sadly, the Love Parade has faced funding and permit issues in recent years and was forced to relocate to other parts of Germany. Unfortunately, the 2009 edition was canceled.

But why did Berlin become the world capital of techno? And why is it still, to this day, the only place where 24/7 clubbing and social activism meet face to face? The cheap standard of living certainly attracted an influx of international DJs and producers. As the city's openly gay mayor Klaus Wowereit put it, Berlin is "poor, but sexy."

After the fall of the Wall, Berliners were determined to build something out of their bleak landscape and found a soul mate in Detroit, with its similar will to survive in the face of decay and historically vibrant DJ and house music culture. Finally, this city of squatters and fringe-livers—particularly communism-blighted East Berlin—was a new frontier with countless empty buildings for the taking. The relationship between the early Berlin pioneers of techno and the techno scene in Detroit remains strong; techno legend Richie Hawtin now calls Berlin his home.

> [top] **Kraftwerk** photo: ©greenplastic875
[bottom] **Hardfloor, Detroit** photo: ©Dave Walk

ART IMITATING LIFE: THE MUSIC IN MOVIES

Tresor Berlin: The Vault and the Electronic Frontier (2004)
Director: Mike Andrawis

We Call It Techno! A Documentary about Germany's Early Techno Scene and Culture (2008)
Directors: Maren Sextro and Holger Wick

High Tech Soul: The Creation of Techno Music (2006)
Director: Gary Bredow

Intellect: Techno House Progressive (2003)
Director: Barclay Crenshaw

Better Living Through Circuitry (1999)
Director: Jon Reiss

Put the Needle on the Record (2004)
Director: Jason Rem

Modulations (1998)
Director: Iara Lee

^ **Watergate** photo: ©Oscar Alexander
‹ **Remains of the Berlin Wall today** photo: ©Aschaf

SEE IT
FOR YOURSELF

Popkomm (Berlin)
Hailed as one of the world's leading music and entertainment trade shows, Popkomm has been taking place since 2004. The related Popkomm Festival brings more than 400 bands to the stages of Berlin's clubs. The next installment of the show and festival will take place in summer 2010.

Detroit Electronic Musical Festival (Detroit)
Held each May on Memorial Day weekend since 2000.

Exit Fest (Novi Sad, Serbia)
Held every year in July at the Petrovaradin Fortress.

photo: ©Veljo Otsason

I Love Techno (Gent, Belgium)
Held in October at the Flanders Expo.

photo: ©Ann Wuyts

We Love Sounds (Throughout Australia)
A winter festival that takes place in June.

Monegros Desert Festival (Fraga, Spain)
Held every year in July.

The story of the club Tresor is emblematic of techno's place in the recent history of Berlin. This underground club (and record label) sprang up in 1991 in the vaults underneath the former Wertheim department store in Mitte, right next to Potsdamer Platz in former East Berlin. The location spoke volumes about the state of Berlin as a squatter's paradise, and the city became a haven for hard techno, industrial, and acid music just a few months after the club's opening. Tresor itself provided a home for DJs from all over Europe, North and South America, and Japan.

Though Tresor maintained its popularity over the years, in a sign of changing times in Berlin, the land it was on was sold to a developer in April 2005. It was reopened in a renovated power plant in Mitte in 2007 and still draws a crowd. Berlin's electronic underground is particularly appealing because for the most part it's unpretentious and open. VIP rooms are basically unheard of, and venues large and small can book the hottest talent. Though bastions of the techno subculture like Pulp Mansion and Sternradio have closed in recent years, and crumbling squats are making way for luxury apartment buildings in certain quarters, Berlin still hosts the largest and most vibrant electronic music community in the world.

> [top] **Bahnhof Potsdamer Platz**
photo: ©Wolfgang Staudt
[bottom] **DJ in action** photo: ©opyh

MAP OF VENUES AND CITY LANDMARKS

1 Berghain/Panorama Bar
Located in a former power plant. Home to some of the hottest electronic music in Berlin—and it has the long lines to prove it!
Am Wriezener Bahnhof
Friedrichshain
+ 2900 0597

2 Cookies
Started out as a weekly event with rotating venues, but has now settled down into a home of its own. Open only on Tuesdays and Thursdays.
Friedrichstrasse/Unter den Linden
+ 2749 2940

3 Delicious Doughnuts
Features a small dance floor and has more of a lounge feel, with scarlet red décor and cozy couches. Check website for techno nights.
Rosenthaler Str. 9
+ 2809 9274

4 Maria am Ostbahnhof
An old, abandoned-looking building full of life on the inside with several bars, dance floors, and a preference for progressive electronic music. Located right beside the River Spree. Famous for its international DJ sets.
An der Schillingbrücke
Friedrichshain
+ 2123 8190

5 Club Tresor
A legend in the Berlin techno scene. Came into being in the early days of Berlin's reunification. Reopened in an old power plant in Mitte in 2007 after the original location was sold. A must-see for real techno lovers.
Köpenicker Straße 70
club@tresorberlin.com

6 Watergate Club
Overlooking the River Spree. Features plenty of electronica spun by local and international DJs. Has a spectacular view of the river.
Falckensteinstr. 49
+ 6128 0395

7 Weekend
Boasts panoramic views of Berlin. Best place to watch the sun come up while local and international DJs spin electronic, pop, and house.
Alexanderstr. 7
+ 2463 1676

8 White Trash
By day, a restaurant with great hamburgers. By night, a bar/club/tattoo parlor with two floors of music. The downstairs is designed like an artificial cave. Entry is free before 8PM.
Schönhauser Allee 6-7
+ 5034 8668

9 Hard Wax
One of the world's leading dealers in the field of cutting-edge electronic dance music.
Paul-Lincke-Ufer 44A
+ 6113 0111

10 Popkomm/ The Station Berlin
Home to one of the world's leading music and entertainment trade shows.
Luckenwalder Straße 4
+ 3038 3009

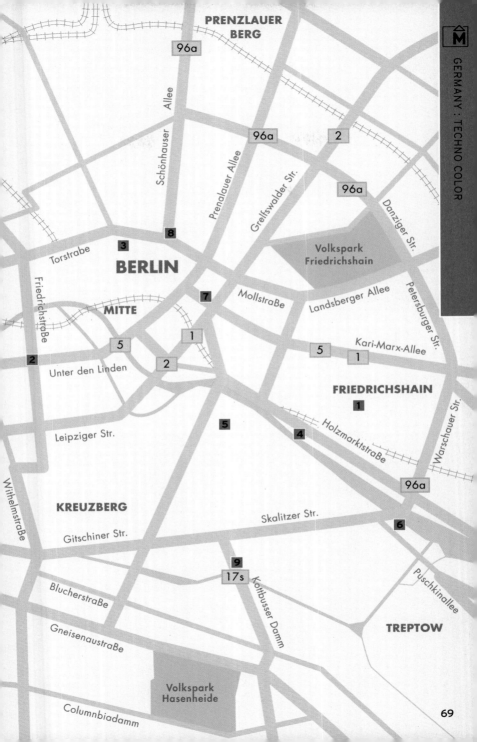

PRENZLAUER BERG

96a

96a   2

96a

Schönhauser Allee

Prenalauer Allee

Greifswalder Str.

Danziger Str.

Volkspark Friedrichshain

8

3

Torstraße

BERLIN

7   Mollstraße

Landsberger Allee

Petersburger Str.

MITTE

Friedrichstraße

5

1

2   2

Unter den Linden

5   1

Kari-Marx-Allee

FRIEDRICHSHAIN

1

Warschauer Str.

5

Leipziger Str.

4   Holzmarktstraße

96a

6

KREUZBERG

Skalitzer Str.

Gitschiner Str.

Puschkinallee

Withelmstraße

9

17s

Blücherstraße

Kotbusser Damm

TREPTOW

Gneisenaustraße

Volkspark Hasenheide

Columbiadamm

69

05: JAILHOUSE ROCK

by Alina Simone

19th c. ▶▶

Tsarist jails breed "criminal chanson" when prisoners combine their own raunchy lyrics with old folk melodies.

1930s–1980s ▶▶

Stalin-era gulags propel the development of chanson. The songs grow more complicated, and become vehicles for political protest.

1991 ▶▶

Fall of the U.S.S.R. Until now, chanson thrived mainly within Russian émigré communities in Paris and New York.

2000s

Today chanson has become the unofficial soundtrack to Russian life. Putin is said to have been a fan of the music as a student, and the Chanson of the Year competition is held in the Kremlin.

Gulf of Finland

● St. Petersburg

● Moscow

●Novosibirsk

North Pacific Ocean

Black Sea

● Astrakhan

Silhouettes of the Moscow Kremlin photo: ©Alexey Bushtruk

The Kazan Cathedral, Moscow

Smolny Cathedral, St. Petersburg

Chizhik Pyzhik, St. Petersburg

Russian "criminal chanson" (or prison music) is a musical reflection of the country's turbulent history of violence and repression.

Born in the Tsarist jails of prerevolutionary Russia, chanson began with prisoners borrowing the minor-key melodies of old folk songs, hymns, or classic Russian "romances" and coupling them with their own bawdy lyrics.

As a genre, it has less in common with field recordings of chain gang spirituals than, say, gangsta rap or the darker side of country music. These songs describe dissolute lives full of ghosts, regret, and malice—men and women struggling to outrun the law or just their own fate. Which is not to say that chanson is necessarily slow or sad. Its coarsest variant, blatnaya muzyca, is loud, obnoxious, and extremely popular with cab drivers (much to the annoyance of just about everyone).

> **Moscow traffic jam** photo: ©Roman Barelko

Moscow

Vladimir Vysotsky Russia's greatest bard, though not technically considered a chanson artist, is known as the voice of a lost generation. Today he remains the most requested artist on Radio Chanson.

Dina Vierny Grew up in Paris and only returned to visit Moscow in the 50s. Afraid to smuggle the written lyrics of banned prison songs back across the border, she committed them all to memory. Vierny's one album, *Songs of the Gulag*, was recorded in Paris and is a classic. photo: ©Pierre Jamet

Gulag Tunes A Moscow-based, art-rock band that creates instrumental surf versions of Stalin-era gulag songs. They are almost as well known for their award-winning album covers as their energetic shows. photo: ©Gulag Tunes

Alexander Galich A successful writer and playwright, who began recording chanson after falling out of favor with Soviet authorities and fleeing Moscow in 1974. From abroad, his songs about life in the camps found their way into Russia via Radio Liberty and quickly became samizdat sensations.

Sergei Trofimov Currently, Moscow's most popular chanson artist; however, some would say his repertoire does not truly embody the folklore of the gulags.

Leonid Utyosov Raised in Odessa but made a home for himself in both Moscow and St. Petersburg over the span of his career. Banned in the 1950s and 60s, and commemorated on Russian stamps today, he is one of chanson's venerable grandfathers.

St. Petersburg

Alexander Rosenbaum This formerly underground artist is now considered mainstream. He even recently served in Parliament as a member of the pro-Putin party United Russia! Perhaps Rosenbaum's most humorous and interesting compositions are those about Odessa's Jewish gangster subculture, many of which are based on stories by Isaac Babel.

Arkady Severny May have been the first artist to use the term "chanson" to describe his chosen genre. The cult sensation managed to record more than 80 albums before his death in 1980.

SEE IT FOR YOURSELF

Chanson of the Year Awards Show (Moscow). Usually held in March in the Kremlin Government Palace.

ALBUMS THAT INFLUENCED CHANSON IN MOSCOW + ST. PETERSBURG

Arkady Severny
Koloda Kart
(Deck of Cards)

Vladimir Vysotsky
Tatuirovka (Tattoo)

Trofim
Aristokratija: Pomoyki
(Gutter Aristocracy)

Aleksandr Novikov
Vezi Menya Izvozchik
(Let's Go Cabman!)

Dina Vierny
Chants du Goulag
(Songs of the Gulag)

Arkady Severny
Fartovy Yad (Lucky Poison)

Arkady Severny i Ansambl Elita
Nochnoy Taxi (Night Taxi)

Bratya Zhemchuzhnye
Mamashi Spyat (Mama's Sleep)

Vladimir Vysotsky
Kupola (Domes)
Rechechka (Tiny River)

Garik Sukachev i Aleksandr Sklyar
Botsman i Brodyaga (A Boatswain and a Tramp)

Villi Tokarev
V Shumnom Balagane (In a Noisy Sideshow)

Lesopoval
Ya Kuplyu Tebe Dom (I Will Buy You a House)

(*NOTE: There are no specific release dates for these albums since originally many of these recordings circulated hand-to-hand as samizdat and were not packaged and sold as albums.)

Perhaps the most vibrant chanson of the prerevolutionary and early Soviet years came from the port city of Odessa, which has its own colorful, Cockney-like dialect. The fading subculture of Odessa's Jewish crime syndicates is immortalized in these jaunty songs that clearly bear the influence of klezmer and gypsy music.

It was in the gulags of the Soviet-era, especially under Stalin, that chanson grew more complicated; seemingly simple songs of banditry and betrayal took on double meanings, becoming vehicles for political protest. Then, during Khrushchev's thaw, a nation in which hardly any family was left unscathed by Stalin's purges embraced chanson and made underground stars out of artists such as the iconic bard Vladimir Vysotsky and the singer Arkady Severny.

Until the fall of the Soviet Union, the exodus of artists to Europe and America created vibrant chanson scenes in Paris and New York's Brighton Beach, where émigré stars like Villi Tokarev still pack them in. Today in Russia, despite persistent complaints that it glorifies violence and criminality, chanson has become the unofficial soundtrack to modern life with its own radio station and television channel. Putin is known to have

> [top] **Russian winter scene** photo: ©Dan Kite
> [bottom] **Moscow city** photo: ©Dmitriy Chistopru

Red Square, Moscow photo: ©Sergey Kelin

been a fan as a student, official monuments to chanson singers abound, and the Chanson of the Year competition is now held in the Kremlin itself.

Because there's nothing like a whiff of death to heighten one's appreciation for prison music, consider making a pilgrimage to Vladimir Vysotsky's grave in Moscow's Vagankovskoye Cemetery. His fans usually gather there on the anniversary of his birth (January 25) and death (July 25) to light candles, sing songs, and commemorate the man known as the voice for a lost generation. Other places to pay tribute include the Theater on Taganka, where the controversial bard-actor once performed the role of Hamlet wearing jeans, the Vladimir Vysotsky Center, which includes relics such as his guitar and costumes, and Vysotsky's monument.

Whether or not you visit Vagankovskoye Cemetery, make a side trip to any major city cemetery in Moscow or St. Petersburg to check out the lavish graves of Russian gangsters.

^ [top] **The outside of Kresty Prison, St. Petersburg** photo: ©Vivian Kam
[bottom] **January 25, 2009 – Vysotsky's birthday** photo: ©Veronica Khokhlova
< **The streets of St. Petersburg** photo: ©Akira Chiba

These men and women were of ill repute and usually paid big bucks for the prime real estate just inside the cemetery gates, so you will not have to walk far to admire elaborate depictions of hit men in track suits, showing off the keys to the new Mercedes. Consider this your illustrated guide to chanson.

You can also have a look at the first head of the KGB, a man whose name was synonymous with the gulag. For decades, Felix Dzerzhinsky's statue terrorized Moscow's Lubyanka Square, but it was torn down by a mob in 1991 and now resides in the Museon, a surreal graveyard of Soviet-era monuments.

In St. Petersburg, a visit to the Kresty Prison (which means "Crosses" because the prison is shaped like a cross) is a great way to get a taste of the suffering from which chanson arose. Built in 1893 and once home to Trotsky and Joseph Brodsky, Kresty is still the city's largest prison. Here you can have a look inside a real solitary confinement cell, check out the prison chapel, and tour a museum featuring inmate art, confiscated shivs, and an exhibit on the symbolism of Russian prison tattoos. There are no guided tours in English (though some are organized by outside tour operators), so bring a Russian friend if you can.

> **Kresty Prison, St. Petersburg**
photo: ©Northfoto

MAP OF VENUES AND CITY LANDMARKS

1 Cafe Club Apshu
An intimate club that looks like a WWII bunker taken over by art students. Occasionally hosts classier chanson acts.
10 Klimentovsky Lane, Moscow + 495 953 9944

2 Cafe Gnezdo Gluharya/ Widgeon's Nest
A well-known restaurant where popular bards perform nightly.
Bolshaya Nikitskaya Ul, 22, Moscow + 495 291 9388

3 Petrovich
Live music club and restaurant housed in the 19th-century basement of a former Cognac factory.
Myasnitskaya 24/3, Moscow + 495 623 0082

4 Taganka Theater
Famous theater known for innovative performances.
Across From Taganskaya Metro Station, Moscow + 495 915 1148

5 Vladimir Vysotsky Center
A museum for the hometown hero, with relics including Vysotsky's guitar and costumes.
3 Nizhny Tagansky Tupik, Moscow + 495 915 7578

6 Art Museon
The surreal graveyard of Soviet-era monuments.
10 Krymsky Val, Moscow + 495 238 3679

7 Kremlin Government Palace
The historic fortified complex at the heart of Moscow. It plays host to the Chanson of the Year Competition.
1 Ulitsa Vozdvizhenka, Moscow + 495 917 2336

8 Korston/Casino De Paris
A swank nightspot—part of a deluxe "Entertainment City" of hotels and clubs. Books top-notch chanson talent. Located in the green district between Vorobyovy Hills and the Moskva River,
Moscow + 495 939 8000

9 Vagankovskoye Cemetery
The site of Vladimir Vysotsky's grave.
Located in Krasnaya Presnya district, Moscow

10 Project OGI Cafe
An underground favorite. The place to catch modern acts with chanson-based repertoires.
Potapovsky Pereulok, 8 Moscow + 495 627 5366

11 Soyuz Record Stores-Moscow
12 St. Petersburg
A Russian music chain with locations in Moscow and St. Petersburg. Good for finding recordings of traditional and modern chanson.
+ 495 589 1551 (Moscow)
+ 812 449 2447 (St. Petersburg)

13 Brodyachaya Sobaka/ Stray Dog
Originally famous as a hangout for anti-establishment luminaries. Now it's an upscale cabaret.
Ploshchod Iskusstv 5/4, St. Petersburg + 812 312 8047

14 Kresty Prison
Built in 1893, and once home to Trotsky and Joseph Brodsky; it is still the city's largest prison.
7 Arsenalnaya Naberezhnaya, St. Petersburg + 812 542 6861

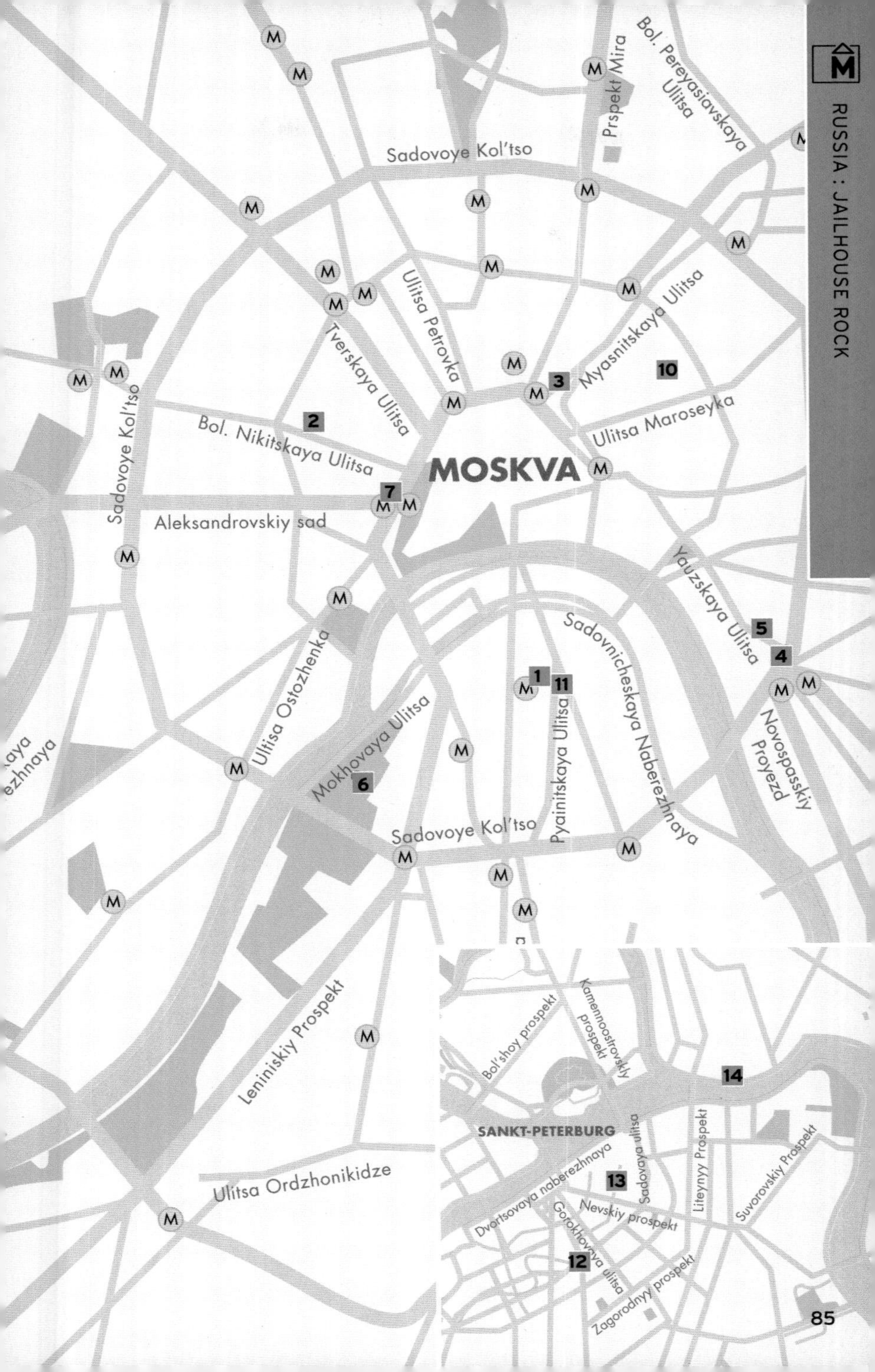

Sadovoye Kol'tso

Prospekt Mira

Bol. Pereyaslavskaya Ulitsa

Ulitsa Petrovka

Tverskaya Ulitsa

Myasnitskaya Ulitsa

Sadovoye Kol'tso

Bol. Nikitskaya Ulitsa

2

3

10

Ulitsa Maroseyka

MOSKVA

7

Aleksandrovskiy sad

Yauzskaya Ulitsa

5

4

Sadovnicheskaya Naberezhnaya

Ulitsa Ostozhenka

1 **11**

Novospasskiy Proyezd

...kaya ...ezhnaya

Mokhovaya Ulitsa

6

Pyainitskaya Ulitsa

Sadovoye Kol'tso

Leniniskiy Prospekt

Ulitsa Ordzhonikidze

14

Bol'shoy prospekt

Kamennoostrovskiy prospekt

SANKT-PETERBURG

Litevnyy Prospekt

Suvorovskiy Prospekt

Sadovaya ulitsa

13

Nevskiy prospekt

Dvortsovaya naberezhnaya

Gorokhovaya ulitsa

12

Zagorodnyy prospekt

06: CLASSICAL STUDIES

by Alexandra Ivanoff

1658 ▶▶▶

Sultan Mehmed IV imports cultural and musical influences from France. Creates a relationship between Western baroque bounty and Eastern desire to become more "cosmopolitan."

Early 1900s ▶▶▶

Heyday of "the Turkish Five," a notable group of classical composers and artists.

1923 ▶▶▶

General Mustafa Kemal Atatürk creates present-day republic of Turkey.

2009

Today there are three major symphony orchestras, two opera houses, three conservatories and numerous active concert venues in Istanbul alone.

Black Sea

Istanbul

● Ankara

Mediterranean Sea

Galata Tower, Istanbul photo: ©Akira Chiba

Night at Beyoğlu

MEPHISTO

Mephisto /Photo
Mephisto

s Sanat photo: ©Mehmet
Çağlarer

Websites:

www.istanbul.net.tr

www.sureyyaoperasi.org

www.iksv.org/english/index.asp

www.klasikmuzik.boun.edu.tr

www.evinilyasoglu.com/ozgecmisi

www.issanat.com.tr

www.akbanksanat.com

www.garajistanbul.org

www.gitarcafe.com

www.bmeia.gv.at/kultur/istanbul/kulturforum/wegbeschreibung.html

Publications:

Cumhuriyet   **Today's Zaman**

Time Out Istanbul

Andante

Turkish Daily News/Hürriyet

If Western classical music is your passion, you won't be disappointed in Istanbul.

Though an ancient city musically and culturally more Eastern for more than a millennium, Istanbul boasts a surprisingly rich contribution to the Western classical tradition, and modern Turks consider classical music of European origin a powerful symbol of the nation's sophistication, history, and uniquely Eurasian identity.

But then, Istanbul has been an exotic blend of East and West since as far back as when they called it Constantinople. Six contemporary Turkish classical musicians who've met with international success exemplify the essence of this blend. Fazıl Say is an extraordinary pianist/composer who headlines around the world; his compositions often use Turkish folk themes in innovative new settings. Kamran Ince, professor of composition at both Istanbul Technical

> **Ortaköy Camii and Bosphorus Köprüsü**
> photo: ©Akira Chiba

HOMETOWN HEROES

From the Past:

Cemal Reşit Rey
photo: ©Evin Ilyasoğlu

"The Turkish Five" composers, all born in the first decade of the 20th century, helped establish Turkey as a viable center of modern music composition.

Opera singers Leyla Gencer and Semiha Berksoy

Pioneer electronic composer Bülent Arel

Legendary Atlantic Records producer Ahmet Ertegün

Composer, pianist, script writer and conductor Cemal Reşit Rey

From the Present:

These six classical musicians (plus Ilhan Mimaroğlu, not pictured) are based in Turkey, but are global performers. They exemplify the essence of what Istanbul has always been: an exotic blend of East and West.

Pianist Idil Biret
photo: ©Idil Biret

Pianist-composer Fazıl Say
photo: ©Marco Borggreve

Violinist Cihat Aşkın
photo: ©Cihat Aşkın

Conductor Cem Mansur
photo: ©Cem Mansur

Composer Kamran Ince
photo: ©Kamran Ince

Electronic composer Erdem Helvacıoğlu photo: ©Erdem Helvacı

ON LOCATION:
ISTANBUL CLASSICAL MUSIC SCENE

Classical music in Istanbul has major venues and outlets to showcase talents, as well as several niche spaces. Here's a list of some of the best spots to check out while you're there:

Major Presenters:
Istanbul State Opera & Ballet

Iş Sanat
Akbank Sanat
IKSV (Istanbul Kültür Sanat Vakfı) Festivals
Borusan Philharmonic
Istanbul State Symphony

Niche Presenters:
Goethe-Institut
Austrian Consulate
Gitar Cafe
Istanbul Recitals
Boğazıçı University
MIAM at Istanbul Technical University

Artists performing at the Topkapi Palace photo: ©Mahmet Ceylan

ALBUMS THAT INFLUENCED CLASSICAL MUSIC IN ISTANBUL

Erdem Helvacıoğlu,
Altered Realities (2007)

Cihat Aşkın
Istanbulin (2007)

Emre Aracı
Sultan Portreleri and "Bosphorus by Moonlight" Violin Concerto (1997)

Leyla Gencer
Bellini: "Beatrice Di Tenda" (1964); and *Bellini: "Norma"* (1964)

Bülent Arel (and various artists)
Pioneers of Electronic Music (2006)

Fazıl Say
Silk Road (and other works) (1994)

Kamran Ince
Symphony No. 3, No. 4, "Domes"/Prague Symphony Orchestra (2005)

Idil Biret
Brahms: Complete Piano Works (2001); and *Rachmaninov: Piano Concertos Nos. 2 & 3* (1998)

University and the University of Memphis (Tennessee), teaches and composes on two continents; *The New York Times* has hailed him as "that rare composer able to sound connected with modern music, and yet still seem exotic." Trained in London, violinist Cihat Aşkın is the winner of many competitions. He specializes in arranging folk music from Turkey and surrounding countries for his Aşkın Ensemble's many recordings of this repertoire. Erdem Helvacıoğlu composes soundscapes that combine electronics and traditional instruments for dance and theatre. Conductor Cem Mansur studied with Leonard Bernstein and has led the prestigious Akbank Chamber Orchestra since 1998. Pianist Idil Biret, a child prodigy in the 1940s, is perhaps the best known of these artists. She received her early training in Paris and has been lauded for decades as an exceptional interpreter of Romantic piano music. She has enjoyed a long international career and still maintains an active concert schedule.

In 1923, General Mustafa Kemal Atatürk created the present republic of Turkey from the ash heap of the dying Ottoman Empire. Part of his strategy to modernize the nation was to promote a cultural exchange with the West, like the wisest of the sultans that preceded him, even personally sponsoring Turkish

> [top] **Concert at Yerebatan Sarmci**
photo: ©Akira Chiba
[bottom] **Kapali Çarsi** photo: ©Akira Chiba

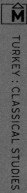

performers' and composers' international tours. A handful of these artists—
"The Turkish Five"—were instrumental in putting Turkey on the Western
classical music map. The most prominent of these was Cemal Reşit Rey,
whose name now graces a major concert hall in Istanbul. After Atatürk heard
soprano Semiha Berksoy sing at the State Opera in 1933, he subsequently
arranged to send her to Germany, where she sang the title role in Richard
Strauss' opera "Ariadne auf Naxos," becoming the first Turkish prima donna
in Europe. Following in her footsteps was Leyla Gencer, a soprano from
Istanbul who enjoyed a long career in Italy, making her U.S. debut at the San
Francisco Opera in 1956. Gencer was known as "La Diva Turca," since her
niche was Italian bel canto roles; in her later years she directed the training
program for young singers at La Scala in Milan, eventually establishing an
international singing competition in Istanbul in her name. Bülent Arel, an
avant-garde electronic music pioneer, worked at the Columbia-Princeton
Electronic Music Center in New York in its early days, then taught at Yale
University and the State University of New York at Stony Brook, whose
studios he designed and built.

Atatürk's cultural exchange with the West wasn't unprecedented among

^ **Dolmabahçe Sarayi** photo: ©Akira Chiba
> **Whirling Dervishes in Sirkeci Station** photo: ©Akira Chiba

Ayasofya Müzesi photo: ©Akira Chiba

SEE IT
FOR YOURSELF

IKSV Klasik Müzik Festival (Istanbul)
Held annually in June and July. One of
the first festivals created in the city. It
celebrates the best of culture and the arts
including classical music, opera, jazz, film,
theater, pop, and more.

photo: ©Pelin Erdogan

Akbank Guitar Festival (Istanbul)
Held annually in March to celebrate the
best artists of classical guitar.

**Leyla Gencer Voice Competition
(Istanbul)**
Held every two years in August, created
in honor of Leyla Gencer. The competition
has garnered international acclaim and
allowed various previous contestants to
move onward to global success.

**Nuri Iyicil International Violin
Competition (Istanbul)**
Held annually in October at the Cemal
Reşit Rey Concert Hall to promote the best
violinists on the contemporary scene.

Siemens Opera Competition (Istanbul)
Held annually in January to promote the
work of talented young opera singers.

the rulers of the 700-year Sultanate
that came before him. A stellar
example is Mehmed IV, Sultan of
the Ottoman Empire during one of
its more enlightened periods (1648–
1687). He commanded from his
bejeweled throne in the gleaming
splendor of Topkapi Palace a
guest troupe of French musicians
and dancers that he had invited
to present musical spectacles for
him. At the same time, Turkish
performers were being welcomed
into the courts of Louis XIV.

As with music education and live
performance in the West, Turkish
classical music is now supported
by banks, public corporations,
private foundations and the
government. The vibrant concert
life of Istanbul, with its many
festivals and competitions,
rivals that of Paris, Berlin, or St.
Petersburg in that it boasts three
major symphony orchestras, two
opera houses, three conservatories,
and numerous chamber-music
and concert venues.

^ **Topkapi Palace** photo: ©Mahmet Ceylan
> **Marmara Sea from Istanbul** photo: ©Akira Ch

MAP OF VENUES
AND CITY LANDMARKS

1 Atatürk Cultural Center
*Includes a large hall with a
capacity of 1300 seats as well
as concert halls, small theaters,
exhibition halls and cinema
spaces. Host to several national
and international activities
and receptions.*
Taksim Square + 312 232 3913

2 Cemal Reşit Rey Konser Salon
*Has a capacity of 550 people and
two large exhibition halls. Belongs
to the Municipality of Metropol
Istanbul. Darülbedayi Caddesi -
Harbiye*
+ 212 232 9830

3 Italian Cultural Center
*Founded to encourage the
promulgation of Italian
language and culture. Organizes
exhibitions, conferences,
concerts, film screenings, and
Italian language courses.*
Mesrutiyet Caddesi No. 75
+ 212 293 9848

4 French Cultural Center
*Founded to encourage the
promulgation of French
language and culture. Often
showcases film screenings and
dance events.*
Istiklal Caddesi 4
+ 212 393 8111

5 Akbank Sanat Beyoglu
*Houses exhibition spaces, a
multi-purpose auditorium, a
dance studio, a music and art
library and a contemporary
art studio. Hosts international
artists, music, and theater.*
Istiklal Cad. No: 8 34435
+ 212 252 3500

6 Garajistanbul
*Arts center that showcases
theater, dance, music
and literature, festivals,
and exhibitions of various
shapes and sizes.*
Tomtom Mah. Yeni Çarcsi Cad.
Kaymakam Resat Bey Sk.
No:11a 34433
+ 212 244 4499

7 Süreyya Opera House
*Designed and built by
the politician Süreyya
Imen Pasha. Originally
established in 1927 as the
first musical theater in the
Western part of Turkey.*
Gen. Asım Gündüz, Cad. 29
+ 216 346 1531

8 Aya·Irini/Hagia Irene
*Located in the Topkapi
Palace grounds, in the
first courtyard behind
the Hagia Sophia.
Features classical music
concerts and art exhibitions
during important
festivals. Serves as a
museum today, but
requires special permission
to visit on certain days.*
Sultanahmet, Eminönü
+ 212 522 1750

9 İş Sanat Kültür Merkezi
*Recognized as the most
prestigious arts and
culture center of Turkey,
this venue often features
a number of artists
that are world-renowned.*
34330 Levent
+ 212 316 1083

HACIAHME

KALYONCUKU

100

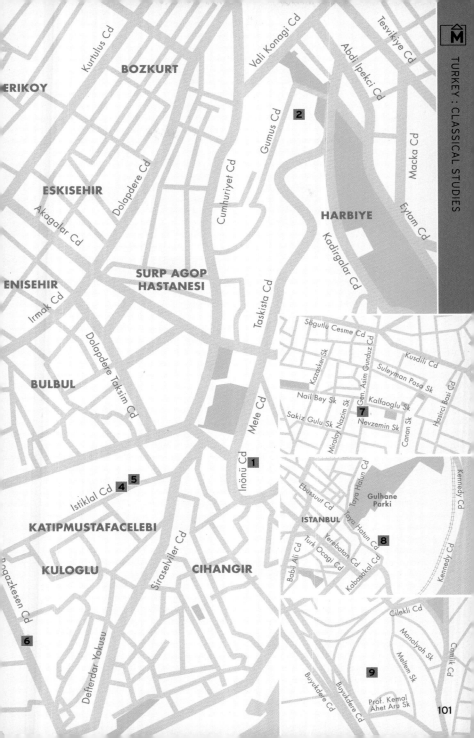

07: SWING SHIFTS

by Mikael Awake

510 ▶▶▶
St. Yared is visited by three birds, which he interpreted as music for the Church.

1950s-1960s ▶▶▶
Addis Ababa's Big Band Era is in full swing and the seeds of Ethiopop are planted. The city is considered a civilized oasis in the heart of darkest Africa.

1970s ▶▶▶
Ethiopia becomes a police state when a brutal Stalinist junta deposes the Emperor Haile Selassie.

1980-1900s ▶▶
Ethiopop re-emerges eschewing traditional instruments in favor of synthesizers and Stevie Wonder riffs.

2009
Ethiopop enjoys international acclaim, drawing from spiritual music, jazz, hip-hop, dancehall and funk.

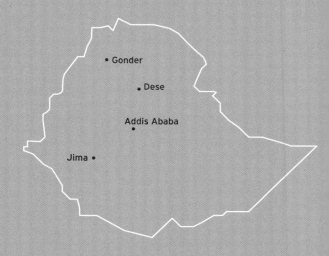

Holy Trinity Church photo: ©Klaas Lingbeek-van Kranen

Ethiopian countryside photo: ©Treestff

Gaslight photo: ©Sheraton Addis, Ethiopia

Ethiopian public bus photo: ©Klaas Lingbeek-van Kranen

When weary travelers step from the terminal at Addis Ababa's Bole International Airport, they are struck by the symphony of sounds. Chants from churches and mosques vibrating in the crisp mountain air; the crowing of roosters and braying of donkeys in the streets; bulldozers clearing a field of rusting shanties for a new office building; teenagers in flip-flops leaning out of minibuses, singing their destinations in quick, rhythmic bursts: Bolé, Bolé, Bolé!

Within this chorus lies the moody, dynamic, captivating world of Ethiopop. A shape-shifting hodgepodge of disparate styles—reggae, hip-hop, mid-century Ethiojazz, synthed-out 80's funk—it's a sound as infectious and cosmopolitan as Addis Ababa itself, a city described by the narrator of Mary Gaitskill's short story, "Don't Cry," as being "of biblical times and modern times, where people walked back and forth between times."

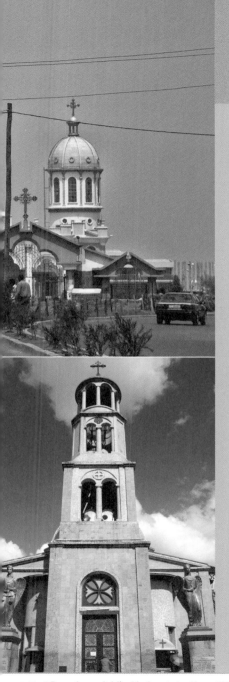

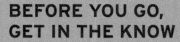
BEFORE YOU GO, GET IN THE KNOW

Websites:
www.afropop.org
www.addistunes.com

Books:
Kay Shelemay
A Song of Longing: An Ethiopian Journey

Films:
***Africa Unite* (2008)**
Director: Stephanie Black
***Broken Flowers* (2005)**
Director: Jim Jarmusch
***Journey to Lasta* (2004)**
Director: Wondwossen Dikran

^ [top] **Downtown Addis Ababa** photo: ©Irene2005
[bottom] **St. Mary's Orthodox Church** photo: ©Robert Bremec

HOMETOWN HEROES

Mulatu Astatke
Beloved composer and xylophonist. Credited as the founder and master of the Ethiopian jazz and pop movement.
photo: ©Alexis Maryon

Ejigayehu "Gigi" Shibabaw
International singing sensation who caught the attention of Island Records' mogul Chris Blackwell in the Jersey City, NJ, backyard of her former manager.
photo: ©Maarten Mooijiman

Mahmoud Ahmed
In every musical tradition, there is always an artist who, over the course of a long and diverse career, manages to remain relevant. In Ethiopop, that person is Mahmoud Ahmed.
photo: ©Damian Rafferty (www.flyglobalmusic.com)

Teddy Afro
The reigning king of contemporary Ethiopop music and its most popular performer. He blends synthed-out reggae beats with more traditional Ethiopian musical styles to form an infectious, charming and widely appreciated body of work. photo: ©Boris Monin

Aster Aweke
Hailing from Gondar, Ethiopia, she is sometimes referred to as "Ethiopia's Aretha Franklin."

Tilahun Gessesse For some Ethiopop enthusiasts, he is, quite simply, the most gifted singer and lyricist to have ever lived.

ALBUMS THAT INFLUENCED ETHIOPOP IN ETHIOPIA

Various Artists
The Very Best of Ethiopiques (2007)

Gigi
Gold and Wax (2006)

Mahmoud Ahmed
Yitbarek (2003)

Rahel Yohannes
Menelik (2003)

Bole 2 Harlem
Bole 2 Harlem, Vol. 1 (2006)

Teddy Afro
Yasteseryal (2005)

Muluken Melesse
Muluken Melesse, Vol. 1 (2008)

Aster Aweke
Aster (1989)

Tilahun Gessesse
Greatest Hits (2000)

Shewandagn Hailu
SK Alegn (2004)

Ethiopian music's walk begins almost 1,500 years ago, in the northern city of Axum, where legend has it that Ethiopian Saint Yared was visited by three birds. A priestly Dr. Doolittle, he understood the birds' songs for what they were: a divine command to write music for the Church. The birds symbolize the Holy Trinity, as well as the three musical modes governing the pensive chanting that remains a hallmark of the Ethiopian Orthodox church service. St. Yared's three birds would later become the inspiration for Bob Marley's song "Three Little Birds."

It's said that St. Yared abandoned courtly life for hermetic meditation in the rugged Semien Mountains, inaugurating the long Ethiopian tradition of music linked to a brooding, melancholy spirituality, a bittersweet ebb and flow of sound that you can still hear in the wistful notes of saxophone legend Getatchew Mekuria (that's him in rapper Common's song "The Game") or the hauntingly beautiful album *Gold And Wax* by international singing sensation Ejigayehu "Gigi" Shibabaw.

Fast-forward the tape deck some 1,400 years, to the heyday of the Big Band Era. In the 1950s and 60s, before Ethiopia became synonymous with famine, drought,

and misrule, Addis Ababa was considered a civilized oasis in the heart of darkest Africa. Its industries thrived, its high culture flourished, and full-color ads in *The New York Times Magazine* touted it as a kind of Paris of the Horn of Africa, a safari destination offering all the comforts of a modern city. An urbanity and youthful exuberance characterized the music and culture of the period, and Addis Ababans wore the same poodle skirts, skinny neckties, cat eyeglasses, and saddle shoes as in the West, even twisting the nights away at dance parties in the Wondo Genet Hotel, which is now shuttered.

After his exposure to African-American music styles—in particular jazz, bebop, and blues— pioneering American-educated composer and xylophonist Mulatu Astatke gave birth to the melodic, complex, and lilting rhythms of Ethiojazz, which would heavily influence Ethiopian music in its wake, including Ethiopop.

In the early 70s, a brutal Stalinist junta deposed the Emperor (and Rastafarian messiah), Haile Selassie, turning Addis Ababa into a police state where musicians were seen as conduits of a decadent and/or American cultural influence.

∧ [top] **Path with a view** photo: ©Robert Bremec
[bottom] **Fans outside of a Teddy Afro concert** photo: ©Alemush

As a result, many musicians were killed, silenced, or forced into exile. Luckily, the greatest works of the pre-Revolution musicians working in Ethiopia were compiled by French ethnomusicologist Francis Falceto in the definitive, 23-volume "Ethiopiques" music series.

During the two decades of Mengistu Haile Mariam's bleak dictatorship, musical innovation more or less came to a grinding halt in Ethiopia. Melodramatic songs of exile and nostalgia (tizita) emerged as a popular form, tallying the losses incurred during the Mengistu years. It wasn't until 1992, after the collapse of communism and the disintegration of his brutal regime, that upbeat Ethiopian pop music got a second chance. Sort of.

The music that re-emerged in the 90s was a far cry from the big band and Ethiojazz sounds, though it took several cues from them. Eschewing traditional instruments in favor of synthesizers, Ethiopop was decidedly less sophisticated fare, slavishly imitating its obvious international influences, even clumsily incorporating things like Stevie Wonder riffs. In the eyes of many purists, Ethiopian music had devolved into a synthetic, mindless simulacrum.

But in the 17 years since the fall of the repressive Mengistu regime, Ethiopop has made great strides, retrieving its heritage and drawing freely from the rich trove of Ethiopian spiritual music (St. Yared's zema) and Ethiojazz while incorporating hip-hop, dancehall, reggae, and funk. Groundbreaking female artists such as Aster Aweke and Gigi have gained widespread recognition in a musical arena formerly dominated by male singers and musicians.

The business of pop in Addis Ababa is very different from the Western model of cutting an album and touring from venue to venue to promote sales and spread the artist's reputation. Instead, venues are associated with artists. Think Bette Midler at Caesar's Palace, except with a quicker (if less predictable) turnaround. An artist will play exclusively at a single venue in association with a particular song. Once the song gets played out, the venue folds.

Hits in Addis Ababa will eventually find their way into nightclubs and restaurants in Washington, D.C., San Francisco, Atlanta, Chicago, and

^ **Man playing African drum** photo: ©OC Photo
‹ **Addis Ababa Dwellings** photo: ©narvikk

Entoto Maryam Church photo ©Robert Brenne

SEE IT
FOR YOURSELF

photo: ©Simon Koo

photo: ©Simon Koo

Mafrika Music Festival (New York City)
Held annually (usually in June) in the outdoor amphitheatre of Marcus Garvey Park. Its mission is to promote African Art & Culture in the United States

ESFNA Soccer Festival (North America)
Taking place in a different major American city every year, the Ethiopian Sport Federation in North America's annual, week-long soccer tournament is the biggest cultural happening in the Ethiopian-American diaspora and an ideal way to soak up the latest in live Ethiopop music. Usually occurs in June and July.

FESPACO (Burkina Faso)
The biannual Pan-African Film and Television Festival, better known as FESPACO, takes place in Ouagadougou, Burkina Faso, and is the largest film festival on the African continent. Usually takes place in March.

Sheba Film Festival (New York City)
The annual event in May, organized by BINA Cultural Foundation Inc, primarily focuses on movies and music that pay homage to the rich legacy of Ethiopian Jews as well as the global Jewish and Ethiopian communities.

other major cities with substantial Ethiopian populations. "This is what everyone's listening to in Addis Ababa," might be something you would hear at D.C.'s Dukem Ethiopian Restaurant where in addition to selling savory helpings of doro wot, you can purchase the latest in Addis Ababa Ethiopop.

Despite the fickle nature of the Ethiopop scene in Addis Ababa, there are several long-perennial venues that any enthusiast should plan to hit, including the rather upscale Gaslight Club at the Sheraton Hotel, where every first Wednesday of the month live jazz sessions are held with two or three guest pop artists. Local radio might be the best way to experience the music while you're visiting. Popular stations include FM 102.1 (locally known as "Sheger"), FM 97.1 ("FM Addis"), and FM 98.3. Perhaps the most famous (or infamous) Ethiopop artist is Teddy Afro (stage name of Tewodros Kassahun), who many believe was targeted by the government for his opposition party anthem "Yasteseryal: Ethiopian History 101" when he was sentenced to six years in prison for the hit-and-run death of a man in May 2008. He is scheduled to be released in October 2009, but critics of the prosecution see the government's imprisonment of Kassahun as another example of Ethiopia slipping back towards authoritarian rule.

Perhaps the true democratic spirit of Ethiopia lies not in the halls of its Parliament but in its music. From the shoeshine boy to the Catholic schoolgirl to the CEO of a multimillion-dollar coffee company, people in Addis Ababa vibrate with music. They know the words to the biggest Ethiopop single of the moment. (Maybe they will forget the words next month, when an even catchier single hits the airwaves, but so what?) They hear it piped out, in tinny bursts, from the blue minivans that race across the city. They hear it jangling softly from the new Bose speakers around the bar of a four-star hotel. They hear it in the banquet halls where a wedding is celebrated, and the bride and groom face each other, their foreheads glistening with sweat and their shoulders shaking fiercely, lovingly, with their iskista moves.

^ **Outside of the Sheraton Hotel** photo: ©Monika Olkowsk (www.rhafurniture.com)

MAP OF VENUES AND CITY LANDMARKS

1 St. Yared Church
A church dedicated to St. Yared (Kidus Yared), known for his contribution to church dance used in worship by Ethiopian Orthodox priests.

2 The Gaslight/Sheraton Hotel
On the first Wednesday of the month, this venue has a live jazz session featuring two or three well-known pop artists. Taitu Street + 517 1717

3 Bole Medhane Alem Church (Holy Saviour)
There's no better place to experience the spirituality of Ethiopian music than a church—and Bole Medhane Alem, the newest, biggest, most lavish church in Addis Ababa, is the best place to do so. Free gigs take place here every Sunday as well.

4 Meskel Square
Meskel Square is a 16-lane junction where all roads meet in Addis Ababa. It's also the site of the Africa Unite concert.

5 Shashemene
The town outside of Addis Ababa where Haile Selassie set aside land for rastas to live. Bob Marley had a house here.

6 Jubilee Palace
Created to commemorate the Silver Jubilee of the coronation of Emperor Haile Selassie I. The park is home to a collection of rare indigenous wildlife.

7 Wondo Genet Hotel
Hotel known in the 50s and 60s for famous dance parties, featuring the best music and culture of the time.

WEREGE

KC

SEBETA

AA

BONEYA

Gaslight Club photo: ©Sheraton Hotel Addis Ababa

(*Note: Many of the venues in Ethiopia do not have specific street addresses. Sometimes they move depending on where the musicians are at. However, you can ask any residents you meet when you get there, and they can give you the rundown on the exact location.)

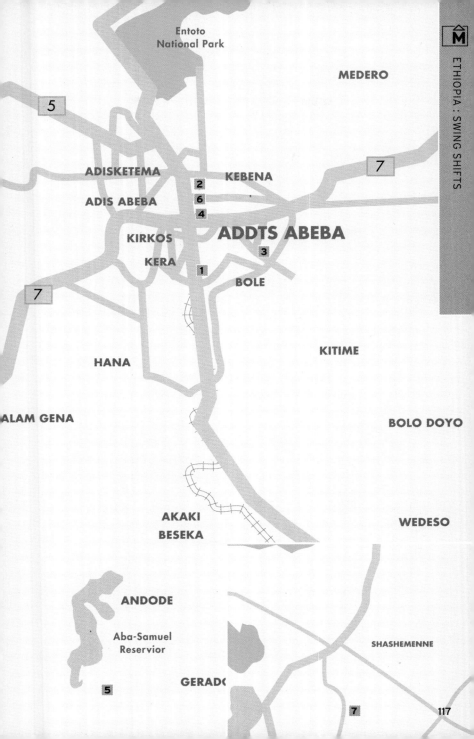

Entoto
National Park

MEDERO

5

ADISKETEMA

KEBENA

7

ADIS ABEBA

2
6
4

ADDTS ABEBA

KIRKOS

3

KERA

1

7

BOLE

KITIME

HANA

ALAM GENA

BOLO DOYO

AKAKI
BESEKA

WEDESO

ANDODE

Aba-Samuel
Reservoir

SHASHEMENNE

5

GERADO

7

08: PASSAGE TO INDIPOP

by Shamik Bag

Early 20th c. ▶▶▶
Ballrooms and city clubs played jazz and opera brought to India by the British.

1947 ▶▶▶
The British leave India, but Western pop music sticks around.

1980 ▶▶▶
Qurbani, a Hindi film, introduces British-Indian music producer Biddu to the mainstream of India's music scene.

1990s
Satellite television keeps the channels of international music alive and growing.

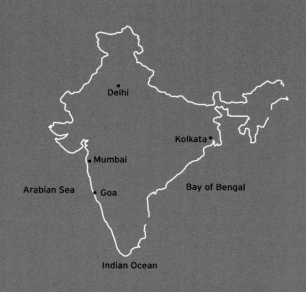

Delhi

Kolkata

Mumbai

Arabian Sea

Goa

Bay of Bengal

Indian Ocean

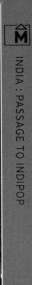

Idol of the Hindu God Ganesha from the Indian festival,
Ganesha Chaturthi, commemorating his birth photo: © Mangesha

Cafe Mondegar photo:
©Suraj Kalot

Tshirt vendor photo:
©Shamik Bag

Streets of Mumbai photo:
©Shamik Bag

BEFORE YOU GO, GET IN THE KNOW

Websites/blogs:

www.gigpad.com
www.rsjonline.com
www.indiecision.com

Magazines:

Rolling Stone India

Blender India

RSJ (formerly Rock Street Journal)

Rave

Chor Bazaar, the name of the bustling flea market in central Mumbai, literally translates to "Thieves' Market." It is a veritable treasure trove of antiques— from Victorian furniture to early 20th-century German fountain-pen nibs to long-playing records. Dusty stacks of LPs line chaotic Mutton Street, where shop owners often vocally volunteer their disdain for the depraved connotation of the market's

name. Flip through scores of Bollywood LPs, till you chance upon an Elvis rarity, a Rolling Stones collectible, or a dog-eared early Beatles album.

While you're at it, maybe you'll find one labeled *Qurbani,* a 1980 Hindi film that introduced the India-born and British-resident music producer Biddu to the mainstream of the Indian music scene. Riding the high tide of disco and an international smash hit in "Kung Fu Fighting," Biddu is widely considered the first to break the cultural "sound barrier" in India with "Aap Jaisa Koi"—his tune in *Qurbani*—a straight-ahead, unmitigated, Western-style pop music confection.

But in fact, long before George Harrison found comfort in the sitar, Kolkata-bred Ravi Shankar performed at Woodstock, Grateful Dead frontman Jerry Garcia's ashes were immersed in the Ganges or Carlos Santana found a Bengali guru in Chinmoy Ghosh, the influence of international pop music was being felt in India.

^ [top] **Wind instrument seller in Colaba** photo: ©Shamik Bag
[bottom] **Taj Mahal Hotel** photo: ©Akira Chiba

Louiz Banks
India's foremost jazz pianist.
Cut his teeth playing with
the likes of Dizzy Gillespie.
photo: ©Louiz Banks

AR Rahman
The genius from Chennai
became known to the world
after two Oscars, a BAFTA,
and a Golden Globe for
Slumdog Millionaire.

Vishal Dadlani
Frontman of the popular rock
band Pentagram. One half of
popular Bollywood composing
duo, Vishal-Shekhar, he brings
with him a distinct sound
ethic. photo: ©Akshayraj Uchil

Shankar-Ehsaan-Loy
The trio of composers who
individually brought Indian
classical, rock, and jazz to
the Bollywood table and
changed the sound for good.
photo: ©Shankar-Ehsaan-Loy

Vijay Nair
The young co-founder of Only Much Louder, India's first rock artist management company and label.
photo: ©Ameet Mallapur

Amit Saigal
Editor of the 16-year-old *RSJ (Rock Street Journal)*, India's first rock music magazine published from Allahabad. An influential force behind the Indian music scene.
photo: ©RSJ

Gary Lawyer
With five solo albums under his belt, Lawyer's deep-set baritone voice has traveled far. As much as the singing, his uncompromising stance towards rock music is well known. photo: ©Gary Lawyer

INFLUENTIAL INDIPOP ALBUMS IN MUMBAI

Louiz Banks
Miles from India (2008)

AR Rahman
Vande Mataram (1997)

Ananda Shankar
Remembering (2008)

Shubha Mudgal
Ab Ke Sawan (2001)

Euphoria
Dhoom (1998)

Usha Uthup
Soundtrack: Shaan (1980)

Pentagram
It's OK, It's All Good (2007)

Shankar-Ehsaan-Loy
Soundtrack: Dil Chahta Hai (2001)

Gary Lawyer
The Other Side of Dawn (1993)

Shaa'ir + Func
Light Tribe (2008)

Colourblind
Self-Titled (2008)

Daler Mehndi
Bolo Ta Ra Ra (1995)

Raghu Dixit Project
Self-Titled (1998)

Rabbi
Self-Titled (2004)

Western sounds hold strongest sway in the country's Northeast region, where turn-of-the-century Christian missionaries charmed tribal communities with the violin when words failed. Of course, the aggressive conversion of the Northeast states involved a lot more than expressive bow-work, but apparently it worked. These days, the Christian-dominated states of Meghalaya, Nagaland, and Mizoram are among the hotbeds of Anglo-American-style rock and pop music, though they otherwise exert only limited influence on mainstream Indian culture.

Mumbai and Kolkata (Bombay and Calcutta, India's most cosmopolitan cities) reverted to their pre-Colonial names in 1997 and 2001 respectively. These coastal seats of British imperial power (Kolkata was India's capital 'til 1911) were likewise among the earliest ports for non-native pop music in India. In the early 20th century ballrooms, the cities' clubs and restaurants vibrated with the sounds of jazz and opera, and the British soldiers and American GIs that passed through during the Second World War brought their swing and big band music with them too. It didn't take long for the English-speaking, Westernized Indian middle and upper classes to develop a taste for these sounds too.

INDIA : PASSAGE TO INDIPOP

Though the British left the country in 1947, Western pop music hung around the urban cocoons of the newly independent nation. But while Bollywood composers like the versatile RD Burman occasionally flirted with Western modes, and shows like *Pop Time* on state-controlled national television pushed pale imitations in the single channel era, Western rock and pop music had relatively little influence on mainstream subcontinental music in the 60s, 70s, and 80s (novelties like "Aap Jaisa Koi" excepted). It wasn't until the 90s, and the coming of satellite television, that British-American rock and pop styles would really strike a lasting chord outside the Anglicized, urban coast, and Northeast states.

Mainstream India, whose exposure to Western-influenced popular music had until then been limited to the state-run Doordarshan television channel's annual deferred telecast of the Grammys, was suddenly bombarded with the stuff, courtesy of MTV India. The channel launched a whole new generation of Indian celebs—Alisha Chinoy, Shweta Shetty, Baba Sehgal, Apache Indian, Suneeta Rao, and Daler Mehndi, the shining stars of "Indipop," a new idiom embracing modernity but sung in Hindi and aimed at a larger demographic than the Anglicized yuppie crowd. As the sound caught on, albums went platinum, and concerts got overbooked and overpriced, leading to the advent of purely manufactured pop bands like Band of Boys and Viva—a mishmash of brawn, cleavage, and vulnerable talent. Indipop began to reel under its own weight.

At Blue Frog, a two-year-old club/studio complex in Mumbai, they're betting that independent bands and musicians can get non-mainstream music back on course, now that it's been demonstrated that there's a mass market appetite in India for music cutting across genres as far-flung as rock, metal, jazz, Indo-Western fusion, electro-funk, punk, minimal house and hip-hop. Also in the game in Mumbai are bars and restaurants like Zenzi, the Hard Rock Café, and Not Just Jazz by the Bay; Haze in Delhi; and Someplace

Else in Kolkata, a decades-old pub and among the first in the country to host daily rock and pop gigs. Websites like gigpad.com and record labels such as Counter Culture promote music that breaks out of the Bollywood-soundtrack formula, completing the picture of the fast-maturing musical subculture crisscrossing young, urban India.

Dhobi Ghat washing slum at Mahalaxmi Station photo ©clearandtransparent

129

SEE IT FOR YOURSELF

Independence Rock (Across India)
One of the oldest rock music festivals in India, I-Rock, as it is known, is ready to step into its 24th year. Held during August and September, the annual festival has included some of the biggest rock bands over the years.

One Tree Festival (Mumbai)
A multi-genre music festival held in February. Previous years have seen the likes of Joe Bonamassa, Robert Cray Band, and Jose Feliciano perform.

Eastwind (New Delhi)
In its inaugural show last year, the organizers promised and delivered three days of music featuring 60 bands performing original songs. You can expect even more in the future.

Congo Square Jazzfest (Kolkata)
Held every winter, this festival has seen performances by veterans like Shawn Lane, Jonas Hellborg, and Karin Krog alongside Amit Heri, Karl Peters, Susheela Raman, and V Selvaganesh.

Joydeb Mela (West Bengal)
Both rustic and chaotic, approximately 2000 Baul musicians gather for a week-long music festival at a small village in the Birbhum district every January. Expect night-long soirees and red-eyed mornings.

Roots Festival (Northeast India)
A springtime festival covering six Northeast Indian states, where musicians travel in a bus and perform original folk, folk-rock and blues music. In recent years, has also seen widespread participation by international bands and artists.

Rock in India (Bangalore)
A festival fashioned along the lines of Rock in Rio, in which international heavyweights like Iron Maiden, Megadeth, Machine Head and Sepultura have rubbed shoulders with numerous Indian rock and metal bands. Usually held in March.

Sunburn Festival 2008 (Goa)   photo: ©Prmod Bafna
Barely two editions old, this festival has created quite a buzz with its Ibiza-styled EDM parties. It features a smattering of the hottest national and international DJs.

A walk down from Mumbai's frantic Churchgate railway station towards Colaba—the south Mumbai neighborhood where bohemian tourism keeps in step with local enterprise amid an architectural mishmash of Victorian, neo-Gothic, and Art Deco buildings—offers tantalizing hints of the penetration of Western music into greater India. In the roadside stalls that line the streets, T-shirts splashed with pictures of Mahatma Gandhi, Om, Frank Zappa and Kurt Cobain hang on the same rack. CDs by Rabbi, Raghu Dixit, Shubha Mudgal and Indian Ocean—among the new crop of artists to find a distinctive Indian voice above the clamor of generic Indipop and derivative rock and metal— are stacked up alongside Buddha Bar, Bollywood, and Backstreet Boys titles. Trumpet, saxophone, hand drum, tin and wooden pipe sellers vie for attention.

Beyond the chic, sanitized environs of the Mumbai nightclubs, in the squalid muddle of Mumbai's Dharavi (the vast sprawl of shanties housing close to an estimated one million people, and made famous around the world by Danny Boyle's Academy Award-winning film, *Slumdog Millionaire*), Sout Dandy Squad, a Tamil rap band, is rehearsing its rhymes—circumspect about the use of too much invective after mentor Apache Indian's word of caution. They sing about the hazards of daily existence in one of Asia's largest slums, even as Mumbai's skyscrapers, sprouting everywhere in a recent construction boom, loom on the horizon, a case study in the contrasts of post-colonial, post-globalized India.

A few miles away, at a central Mumbai bar, evenings aren't the same since the local government put a blanket ban on girls dancing for the entertainment of customers. Like scores of former "dance bars" in Mumbai, it has reinvented itself as an "orchestra-singing bar," where the girls are allowed to sing off-key but not shake a leg.

The dimly lit, reverberating interiors can't hide the mediocrity of the performance as the sari-clad singer does battle with some old-school Bollywood classics. Changing tracks, she launches into a rendition of "Socha Hai," from the recent Bollywood hit *Rock On!!*, which firmly stamped rock music on the wider public consciousness. She follows it up with a version of "Made in India," a foot-stomper that catapulted Indipop singer Alisha Chinoy into the high heavens of celebrity. As the middle-aged audience gamely joins in on the chorus, Mumbai's midnight turns crimson evening again.

^ **Mumbai signs** photo: ©Shamik Bag

MAP OF VENUES
AND CITY LANDMARKS

1 Rhythm House
*Over half a century old,
Mumbai's biggest repository
of music features a vast
collection of music across
multiple genres.*
40, K Dubash Marg
+ 4322 2727

2 Furtado's
*Over 140 years in the music
business. A one-stop shop
for musical instruments,
both Indian and foreign, and
albums by Indian rock
and metal bands.*
540-44, Kalbadevi Road
+ 6622 5454

3 Mini Market
*A store that commands
a respectful presence in
Mumbai's Chor Bazaar. Offers
reproductions of classic
Bollywood posters and rare
Indian and Western LPs.*
33/31 Mutton St.
+ 2347 2427

4 Not Just Jazz by the Bay
*Good food along with a great
view of the Arabian sea and a
wide choice of live music.*
143, Soona Mahal, Marine Dr.
+ 2285 1876

5 Blue Frog
*With a daily gig schedule,
exclusive ambience, and
exhaustive menu, this is
where the hip and happening
of Mumbai unwind.*
Mathuradas Mills Compound
NM Joshi Marg, Lower Parel
+ 4033 2300

6 Café Mondegar
*"Mondy's" to regular patrons,
the Café, situated right at
the entrance to Colaba, is*

*a big draw among those
looking to down a few beers
accompanied with music from
the retro jukebox.*
Metro House, Shahid Bhagat
Singh Road, Apollo Bunder
+ 2202 0591

7 Toto's Garage
*A popular hangout that
features great music and
good spirits.*
30, Lourdes, Pali Junction
Bandra West
+ 2640 6429

8 Ghetto Pub (The)
*An alternative, underground
bar and club for the rock-
loving crowd. Located behind
the Mahalaxmi Temple.*
30, Bhulabhai Desai Road
+ 2353 8418

9 Soul Fry Restaurant
*A well-known restaurant
serving excellent seafood
amid a friendly, social scene.*
Silver Croft, Pali Market,
Pali Mala Road, Bandra West
+ 2604 6892

10 Chor Bazaar
*This renowned, bustling
flea market is located in
central Mumbai.*
Mutton St. Mandvi

11 St. Peter's Boys School
*Located 280-odd kms from
Mumbai. The school where
Farrokh Bulsara (Freddy
Mercury of Queen) studied,
learned to play the piano, and
formed a band. Continues
to have a culture in sound
music training.*
Panchgani, Satara District
Pin - 412 805, Maharashtra
+ 2168 241584

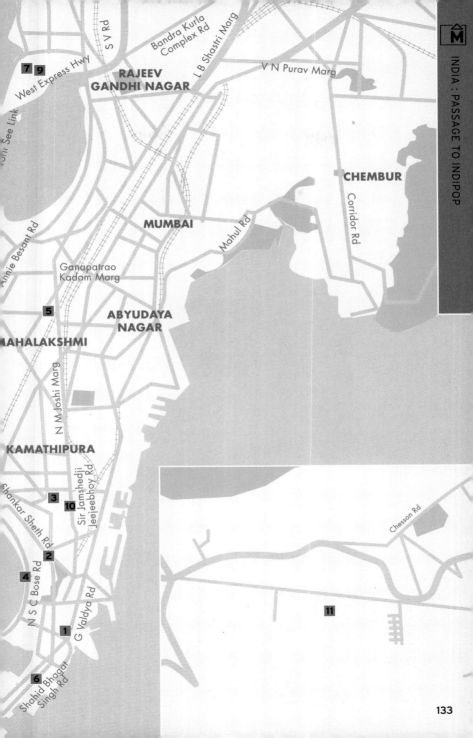

7 **9**

West Express Hwy

S V Rd

Bandra Kurla
Complex Rd

L B Shastri Marg

V N Purav Marg

**RAJEEV
GANDHI NAGAR**

ihii See Link

CHEMBUR

Annie Besant Rd

MUMBAI

Mahul Rd

Corridor Rd

Ganapatrao
Kadam Marg

5

**ABYUDAYA
NAGAR**

MAHALAKSHMI

N M Joshi Marg

KAMATHIPURA

Sir Jamshedji
Jeejeebhoy Rd

Shankar Sheth Rd

3

10

Chesson Rd

2

N S C Bose Rd

4

11

G Valdya Rd

1

6

Shahid Bhagat
Singh Rd

09: EXPERIMENTAL METHODS

by Nick Frisch

1970s ▶▶

China cracks a door open to the rest of the world and foreigners start smuggling in Rolling Stones and Frank Zappa tapes.

1986 ▶▶

Cui Jian plays "Nothing to My Name" on a TV special and becomes the first public example of a successful musician not sponsored by state.

1989 ▶▶

Tiananmen Square demonstrations. The world is shocked by the violent images shown on TV.

2000s ▶▶

China's underground pop music grows into a formidable above ground scene.

2008

Beijing hosts the Olympics. The world is impressed.

Beijing ●

Pacific Ocean

Shanghai ●

South China Sea

Figures of soldier and horses, clay, photo: ©kladkhoon

Entrance to Yugong Yishan
photo: ©Yugong Yishan

MAO
live house
鼓楼东大街111号

Mao live house photo:
©Philip Jägenstedt

Jeffray Zhang Shouwang
with Simon Frank at D-22
photo: ©Nick Frisch

D-22

BEFORE YOU GO, GET IN THE KNOW

Websites:

www.yanjun.org

www.ent.sina.com.cn

wiki.rockinchina.com

www.newmusicchina.org

www.pentatonicworkshop.org

www.yaogun.com

Magazines:

So Rock! Magazine

Muse Magazine (Hong Kong)

That's Beijing

The Beijinger

"Crossing the river by feeling for stones" was a favored catchphrase of Chairman Mao Zedong's successor, Deng Xiaoping. Ever since the passing of Mao, a China of ideological extremes has yielded to experimentation and pragmatism in economics, academics, and especially, the arts.

Though Beijing's politicians are as entrenched as ever, artists have flourished in the capital of late, largely untouched by censorship and free to discover new things through trial and error.

The contemporary art scene, focused around the 798 Art Zone in the city's northeast, has become an international sensation thanks to its *enfants terribles*' recycling of Communist themes. The city's musical landscape, however, remains a lesser known and evolving gem— a "weird-ass petri dish" in the

> **Beihai** photo: ©JackVersloot

HOMETOWN HEROES

Eli Marshall
The founder and conductor of the Beijing New Music Ensemble, Marshall first came to Beijing on a Fulbright fellowship in 2003. Marshall has been spotted occasionally at D-22 and the now defunct OT Lounge, adding his keyboard improvisations to the night's music.
photo: ©Candice Kwan

Leon Lee Baoyan
Jack-of-most-trades, Lee emerged from a thicket of awards and honors in the American arts world to lend his PR-savvy touch to some local venues. Along the way, he brought Brazilian drumming and non-profit arts management know-how to Beijing.
photo: ©Leon Lee Baoyan

Jeffray Zhang Shouwang
The face that launched a thousand breathless articles, Zhang, the wunderkind of Beijing rock, has flourished with D-22 as his base and Michael Pettis as his patron. Between his more traditional band, Carsick Cars, and his experimental two-person project, White, he is easily the most famous young musician on the Beijing scene today.
photo: ©Philip Jagenstedt

Michael Pettis

Banker by day and rock-club owner by night, Pettis lived a double life in New York—and brought it with him to Beijing. He opened D-22 in 2006 and has established himself as an emerging markets authority on his blog and a professor at Peking University.
photo: ©Matthew Niederhauser (mdn@mdnphoto.com)

Yan Jun

A cerebral polymath, Yan Jun programs the celebrated Tuesday night series of avant-garde music at 2 Kolegas, while running a blog, keeping up a steady stream of music criticism, and maintaining his own career as a sound artist. photo: ©Yan Jun and Contemporary Art + Music Magazine

Wu Na

A 1991 graduate of the Central Conservatory of Music, Wu Na is one of the most accomplished qin players of her generation, beloved to traditionalists and avant-garde fans alike. Her bending, sinewy pitches often join other experimental musicians in Beijing and elsewhere. She's appeared during the once-legendary OT Lounge jazz/experimental nights at the Oriental Taipan Bakery.
photo: ©Weilin Wang

LANDMARK ALBUMS OF EXPERIMENTAL MUSIC IN BEIJING

10
Nomad (2008)

FM3
*The Buddha Machine (*not actually an album, but a music box)* (2008)

Li Jianhong
Bird (2007)

Beijing New Music Ensemble
Wild Grass (2009)

Carsick Cars
Self-Titled (2007)

Xiao He
*2009 Europe Tour (*not yet titled or released)* (TBD)

White
Self-Titled (2008)

Wang Fan
Sound of Meditation Within the Body (2001)

Various Artists (compiled by Yan Jun)
Noise is Free (2008)

Miquia
Sign Language (2005)

words of Beijing-based composer Eli Marshall. Former Bear Stearns trader Michael Pettis, who relocated from New York to Beijing in 2002, is betting the city will play a big role in the new music of the 21st century. Now an influential club owner and blogger, he's on the record claiming Beijing among the "top five or ten cities in the world for music" and working hard to make that characterization a reality.

So what brings Westerners like Marshall and Pettis here? Foreign artists find Beijing affordable and freewheeling and often revel in finding creative freedom in a country with such an authoritarian reputation. Beijing has long been the nation's unchallenged capital of culture. Even during the Cultural Revolution—when the state's totalitarian grip was weakened by political upheaval—the arts were still dictated from Beijing, reduced under the iron-fisted control of Mao's wife, Jiang Qing, to revolutionary formulas like the "eight model plays." And the cityscape is as diverse as any in LA or Berlin. A vast expanse of grit encompasses old and new: should you choose, you can find isolation or inspiration in hutong alleyway neighborhoods dating back hundreds of years, or a slick ultramodern neighborhood whose history stretches back no further than the 2008 Olympic Games.

> **Japanese-Korean duo 10 show off the Beijing scene's international flavor during a jam at 2 Kolegas** photo: ©Nick Frisch

Visitors to Beijing can peek in on an evolving music scene that exemplifies the broader meaning of "experimental." Here, musicians constantly push boundaries and try new things, picking and choosing, and mixing, cutting, and remixing. African DJs, American classicists, Brazilian drummers, and Japanese computer musicians come here for the low overhead and welcoming venues. They mix and mingle with local Chinese musicians, who themselves are free to pick and choose whether they want to approach Beijing as a place to work within the vast tradition of Chinese music, or as a neutral meeting ground for global influences, or somewhere in between.

As China cracked a door open to the outside world in the late 70s, the first great musical challenge was to do anything at all free of the supervision of the state, from smuggling in Rolling Stones and Frank Zappa tapes to writing and playing songs free of political or cultural orthodoxy. A few early foreigners trickled in as well, bringing recordings and skills along with path-breaking careers in diplomacy, business, or academia. And one young man—an ethnic-Korean Chinese named Cui Jian—moved from trumpet to guitar, sang one song during a TV special in 1986, and became the first public example of a musician making it big outside the strictures of the state. The breakout hit was "Nothing to My Name," and despite a bumpy artistic road through the 1989 Tiananmen crackdown (when Cui had to leave town for a while), his example of mixing Western rock with Chinese harmonies became an oft-copied model. A trickle of musical exposure became a deluge as whole decades of 20th-century musical history, so long withheld from China's cultural scene, flooded into Beijing and mixed with predictably interesting results.

Slowly, more experimenters joined the ranks, and bands and venues sprouted across Beijing, with one Wang Fan widely credited for making the rock-to-experimental jump. Many bands were—and still are—derivative copiers of Western idioms, but Beijing's cheap lifestyle and density of culture have attracted enough talent to start a true artistic conversation. As China vaulted into the world's consciousness in the mid-2000s, a few venues rose from "local dive" status to become citywide institutions; meanwhile, local musicians started to garner attention abroad, with up-and-coming artists such as Jeffray Zhang Shouwang taking trips to New York to meet musical luminaries.

Now, scenesters come to shows bristling with expensive recording devices to capture every moment of performances, and debates rage in English and

143

2008 Olympic Games National Stadium (Bird's Nest) and night traffic in Beijing photo ©iPhotos

SEE IT
FOR YOURSELF

Midi Festival (Beijing)

An annual festival traditionally held in May for experimental music, in both the broad and formal senses of the word. Rock, punk, classical, and electronic music converge and collide with no obeisance required to any prior tradition or milieu. Recent years have seen the date and location change, so check ahead.

Mini Midi Festival (Beijing)

An offshoot of the Midi Festival, it occurs at the same time. Organized and run by the owners of the club 2 Kolegas, it is the only outdoor event for experimental music in China.

photo: ©Ian Holton

Chinese about whether locally bred originality has overwhelmed imported imitations. There is a China rock wiki (http://wiki.rockinchina.com) and *The New York Times* has even weighed in on Chinese hip-hop and electronica. Still, the music scene has avoided the gentrifying spotlight that brought a boutique hotel and fine French dining to the 798 Art Zone. 2 Kolegas, Beijing's premiere venue for experimental music, is a gritty shack situated on the edge of a drive-in theater complex.

The annual Midi Festival in May has made ample room for experimental music, in both the broad and formal senses of the word. Numerous shows in all styles—Brazilian drum troupes, Mongolian rock groups, flamenco played by Muslim Uighurs from China's northwest—happen in any given week. Rock, punk, classical, and electronic music converge and collide with no obeisance required to any prior tradition or milieu (try pulling that in Berlin). But there's always the cultural richness and depth of China for those who choose to orient their work around it. Whether you lament Beijing music's relative immaturity or get excited over its evolving potential, you certainly won't be bored.

> [top] **The Forbidden City** photo: ©joebrandt
> [bottom] **Tiananmen Square** photo: ©Brian Jeffery Beggerly

中华人民共和国万岁　世界人民大团结万岁

2009 marks the 20th anniversary of the Tiananmen Square protests of 1989, when the world watched in horror as supporters of Hu Yaobang (a pro-market, prodemocracy, and anti-corruption official) took to the streets to mourn his passing and ended up facing violent suppression from the government of the People's Republic of China, resulting in injuries or death for thousands of Chinese citizens.

MAP OF VENUES AND CITY LANDMARKS

1 **2 Kolegas/Waterland Kwanyin**
Yan Jun's brainchild. The site of the iconic Tuesday night Waterland Kwanyin event, Beijing's most regular experimental showcase.
21 Liangmaqiao Lu
+ 6436 8998

2 **Yugong Yishan**
Recently relocated to a traditional hutong setting and books an eclectic mix of DJs, bands, Brazilian drummers, and others.
3-2 Zhangzizhong Lu
+ 6404 2711

3 **D-22**
A major incubator for Beijing's bands and music. Its distance from the city center—far out in the university district— belies its artistic centrality.
242 Chengfu Lu
+ 6265 3177

4 **MAO Live House**
Has a decidedly punk-rock focus. Nonetheless, attracts its share of forward- thinking experimenters.
11 Gulou Dong Dajie
+ 6402 5080

5 **Central Conservatory of Music**
Highly respected, leading musical institution in China.
43 Baojia Lu
+ 6605 3531

6 **Sugar Jar Record Shop**
Underground music store known for its broad selection of independent Chinese music.
2 Jiuxianqiao Lu
+ 6433 1449

7 **Workers' Stadium**
City landmark stadium that plays host to major events, including the legendary 1986 Cui Jian performance of "Nothing to My Name," and competitions during the 2008 Olympics.
Gongti Bei Lu
+ 6669 9185

8 **798 Art District**
Home of Beijing's thriving art community, located among 50-year-old decommissioned military factory buildings.
Jiuxianqiao Lu,
Chaoyang District

9 **Jiangjinjiu Bar**
An intimate space that offers laid back jam sessions. It often hosts ethnic minority bands, usually with no cover charge.
2 Zhongku Hutong
+ 8405 0124

10 **Jimmy's Thai Kitchen & Lounge**
A new 100-seat capacity music venue that presents jazz, world, blues, soul, rhythm & blues, folk, funk, and new music.
Dongzhong Jie
East Gate Plaza Tower B 1/F
+ 6415 5157

N 5th Ring Rd

Chengfu Rd

3

Subway Line 4 (Under Construction)

Zhichun Park

N 3rd Ring Rd E

Beijing Z

Subway Line 1

Olympic Park

N 5th Ring Rd

Beijing Chaoyang
Wangjing Park

6

Jiuxianqiao Rd

Madian Park

N 3rd Ring Rd East

Subway Line 2

1

Liangmaqiao Rd

Houhaibeiyan

Beiluogu Alley

8

4

Di'anmen East St

2

10

7

XinDong Rd

Beihai Park

Guangqumennantinhe Rd

9

Temple of Sun Park

**CHAOYANG
DISTRICT**

BEIJING

Subway Line 2

E 3rd Ring Rd North

**CHONGWEN
DISTRICT**

Taoranting Park

Subway Line 5

Amusement
Park of Beijing

149

AUSTRALIA - MELBOURNE, SYDNEY + BRISBANE

10: ART ROCK CONFIDENTIAL

by Mel Campbell

1970s ▶▶▶
Art rock community begins growth on campus radio. The Saints release what is widely hailed as the world's first "punk" record.

1986 ▶▶▶
Richard Lowenstein's film *Dogs in Space*, starring Michael Hutchence of INXS, presents a fictionalized account of the "little bands"/ art rock scene.

1991-2005 ▶▶▶
Meredith Music Festival (1991) and St. Jerome's Laneway Festival (2005) begin annual traditions of celebrating art rock out in the open.

2006 ▶▶▶
Mistletone Records is founded by Ash Miles and Sophie Best to distribute art rock records and present tours of internationally known artists.

2009
Nick Cave programs the first Australian All Tomorrow's Parties Festival, bringing art rock to the masses on a global scale.

Melbourne, Australia photo: ©I.mapoJ

Rocking Horse Records photo:

Sydney photo: @oksana.sto

The Toff photo: ©The Toff

@Rocking Horse Records

Rocking Horse

Australia has always keenly felt its isolation from the rest of the world, and its art rockers have historically drawn support and inspiration from each other rather than striving to branch outward along conventional industry trajectories to success. To appreciate this experimental, lo-fi music, you've got to go where it's happening.

The southern city of Melbourne, historically one of Australia's most cosmopolitan, is the current art rock capital. But the scene's roots are in the sunny northern city of Brisbane. Under ultraconservative state premier Joh Bjelke-Petersen (who resigned in 1987, after 19 years in office, as a result of a high-level corruption scandal), Brisbane was Australia's least sophisticated and most politically repressive metropolis.

In 1976, Brisbane punk band The Saints independently recorded and distributed their debut single "(I'm) Stranded," which has since been widely hailed as the world's first punk record. The Saints' spontaneity and do-it-yourself approach inspired a multitude of other post-punk Melbourne acts.

BEFORE YOU GO, GET IN THE KNOW

Websites:

www.whothehell.net
www.messandnoise.com
www.arena.

Magazines:

The Monthly

Cyclic Defrost
(Issue 22 cover design, ©We Buy Your Kids 2009)

Films:

Dogs in Space (1986)
Director: Richard Lowenstein

Sticky Carpet (2006)
Director: Mark Butcher

^ [top] **Melbourne beach in summer** photo: ©Nicole Paton
[middle] **Brisbane city lights** photo: ©Quirex
[bottom] **The Toff** photo: ©The Toff

HOMETOWN HEROES

Aleks and the Ramps
Originally from Canberra, but are now based in Melbourne. A huge cult favorite, the band's also garnered a fair amount of international acclaim.
photo: ©Aleks and the Ramps

Guy Blackman
Originally from Perth, he's a journalist and anti-folk musician who also runs indie record label Chapter Music. Through this label, Blackman has reissued on CD the few recordings from Melbourne's "little bands" scene of the 70s.
photo: ©Guy Blackman

Nick Cave
An internationally famous singer-songwriter known for his early work with The Birthday Party, and later with the Bad Seeds and Grinderman. Cave programmed the first Australian All Tomorrow's Parties Festival in 2009. photo: ©Marco Annunziata

Robert Forster
A Brisbane-based musician and award-winning music reviewer for the Australian magazine *The Monthly*. Forster co-founded the internationally acclaimed indie-pop band The Go-Betweens and has released five solo albums. photo: ©Andy Gotts, 2008

Ben Gook
A music journalist (for *Mess + Noise*), photographer, and bassist with the band Deloris, now based in Berlin. Literary magazine *Arena* recently hailed Gook as "Australia's best young music critic."
photo: ©Mess + Noise

Matthew Levinson
A Sydney music journalist, DJ, radio broadcaster and co-editor of *Cyclic Defrost*, a magazine of independent Australian electronica.
photo: ©Matthew Levinson

Woody McDonald
Until March 2009 , he was the music director at Melbourne community radio station RRR. McDonald also books bands for the Meredith and Golden Plains music festivals. photo: ©Woody McDonald

Mistletone Records
An independent label founded in 2006 by Melbourne couple Ash Miles and Sophie Best. In addition to key Australian art rock artists, Mistletone distributes records and presents tours by internationally known artists. It also hosts quarterly mini-festivals in several Australian cities.
photo: ©Jonathon Bailey

Leith Thomas
A noise and hardcore bassist, former publisher of independent magazine *What We Do Is Secret* (now defunct), and cofounder of specialist noise label Sabbatical Records. photo: ©Tim Hillier

ALBUMS THAT INFLUENCED ART ROCK IN AUSTRALIA

Essendon Airport
Sonic Investigations of the Trivial (2002)

The Birthday Party/Boys Next Door
The Birthday Party (1980)

The Saints
(I'm) Stranded (1977)

The Go-Betweens
Liberty Belle and the Black Diamond Express (1986)

Primitive Calculators et al
Primitive Calculators and Friends (2007)

Hand Hell
Phonography (2007)

Fabulous Diamonds
7 Songs (2008)

Aleks and the Ramps
Pisces vs. Aquarius (2007)

Kes Band
The Grey Goose Wing (2007)

True Radical Miracle
Cockroaches (2006)

Some, such as the Primitive Calculators, Essendon Airport, The Birthday Party, and Whirlywird, went on to relative notoriety; others lasted only a single show.

These "little bands" were far more adventurous with their instrumentation than practitioners of the riff-based "pub rock" sound, which dominated at the time. They incorporated synthesizers and their songs reflected classical, jazz, and world music influences. Contemporary Aussie art rock still regards music-making as a spontaneous, hands-on process, attaching great prestige to unlicensed or temporary venues and performances that emphasize onstage theatrics rather than technical virtuosity.

Recordings are independently produced, distributed, and funded by many tiny labels often run by the bands themselves. Bands sell their recordings at shows, online, or through independent record stores. In Melbourne, Missing Link Records specializes in alt-rock, punk, and hardcore; Polyester Records and newcomer Title Music also stock plenty of obscure bands. Other retailers include Red Eye Records in Sydney, Rocking Horse Records in Brisbane and 78 Records in Perth.

> [top] **The Tote** photo: ©The Tote
> [bottom] **Concert goers at a Melbourne festival, sponsored by Triple J** photo: ©Brad

While they tour regularly and have loyal niche followings, few art rock musicians earn enough money to make a living from performing. Hence, most are also journalists, publicists, and event managers. Musicians run labels, work in record stores, or tend bar at venues. Those on the scene's geographic fringes in Perth, Adelaide, Canberra, and Hobart regularly travel to its centers of Melbourne, Brisbane, and Sydney.

This creates a tightly knit and self-sufficient scene whose musicians are more prone to collaborate and converse with each other than seek to "break out." In fact, many bands actively repel mainstream interest.

The inner-urban cityscape is their key space of inspiration and performance. Being a knowledge-rich but cash-poor pursuit, art rock is pursued by bands that naturally migrate to areas with cheap housing and large student populations. In Australia, most students don't live on campus, so social and creative life happens in bars ("pubs") and at house parties.

A thriving network of idiosyncratic music festivals supports the scene. The Meredith

---

^ [top] **Rocking Horse Records** photo: ©Rocking Horse Records
[bottom] **The Meredith Music Festival** photo: ©Mandy Hall
‹ **Pony** photo: ©Pony

A Melbourne laneway photo: ©Marco Bueno de Moraes

SEE IT
FOR YOURSELF

Golden Plains Festival photo: ©Mandy Hall

Meredith Musiç Festival (Victoria)
Since 1991, this festival has traditionally been held every year in December on a farm northwest of Melbourne, with acts ranging from emerging locals to forgotten legends and international indie stars.

Golden Plains (Victoria)
Started in 2007 as a sister festival to Meredith, this festival takes place on Labour Day Weekend in March and features similar acts to Meredith.

Applecore (Melbourne)
Traditionally held in February, this one-day festival takes place in a suburban backyard and showcases obscure bands.

Cherry Rock (Melbourne)
A festival, usually held in April, that features a line-up of local garage-rock acts playing in the laneway outside Melbourne's iconic Cherry Bar.

The St. Jerome's Laneway Festival (Melbourne)
A national touring festival, with acts ranging from art-rock locals to international guests. Traditionally held in February–March.

Music Festival has been held since 1991 on a farm northwest of Melbourne, with acts ranging from emerging locals to forgotten legends and international indie stars. In 2007, it sprouted a sister festival, Golden Plains, which in 2009 was headlined by Gary Numan.

Applecore is a one-day Melbourne festival held annually in a suburban backyard and showcasing extremely obscure bands, while the Cherry Rock festival features a line-up of local garage-rock acts playing in the laneway outside Melbourne's iconic Cherry Bar.

On a larger scale, the St. Jerome's Laneway Festival is now a national touring festival, with acts ranging from art rock locals to international guests. It's such a success that when Girl Talk headlined in 2009, many art rock fans were up in arms, feeling the festival had abandoned the

grassroots spirit of the original 2005 event, in which unsigned bands played in the laneway outside the namesake Melbourne bar.

Independently published magazines and blogs act as important brokers of the art rock community, as does public radio. Australian community radio stations grew out of campus radio in the 1970s and are staffed by volunteers and funded by subscriptions from listeners and local businesses. Key stations are RRR (102.7 FM) and PBS (106.7 FM) in Melbourne, FBi (94.5 FM) and 2SER (107.3 FM) in Sydney, RTR (92.1 FM) in Perth, and ZZZ (102.1 FM) in Brisbane.

Many community radio presenters graduate to Triple J, the government-funded national youth radio network. When it was first founded in the 1970s, Double Jay, as it was then known, "broke" radio-unfriendly acts like the

Clash, but these days it's thought of more as a mainstream station for teenagers.

Sydney journalist Dom Alessio is the current host of Triple J's local music show, "Home And Hosed," based largely on the popularity of *Who The Bloody Hell Are They?* (www.whothehell. net), a blog he started with Melbourne band manager Jerry Soer in 2006. *Who The Hell?* is dedicated to new Australian music and currently edited by Soer.

Another key media outlet is *Mess+Noise* (www.messandnoise.com). Founded as a free magazine dedicated to independent Australian music, it's now a website specializing in very long features and polemics. Its online forum is a snarky space for art rock musicians and fans to chat—so much so that its users are colloquially known as "chats."

Australian art rock is sufficiently underground to have escaped much historical documentation, but it's worthwhile seeking out the 1986 film *Dogs in Space,* Richard Lowenstein's fictionalized representation of the "little bands" scene, starring Michael Hutchence of INXS. The 2006 documentary *Sticky Carpet* also features live performances and interviews from many key art rock players, and the 2009 Melbourne International Film Festival had a programming stream dedicated to post-punk in Melbourne.

ᴧ **Golden Plains Festival** photo: ©Mandy Hall
‹ **Graffiti art from Caledonian Lane** (former home of St. Jerome's Bar/Laneway)
  photo: ©Ben Britten

MAP OF VENUES
AND CITY LANDMARKS

1 The Toff In Town
Intimate, cabaret-style venue that suits a wide variety of acts. Favors art rock in its programming choices.
252 Swanston St.,
Melbourne + 9639 8770

2 Pony
Grungy all-night rock bar known for its adventurous live programming and 2AM headline slots.
68 Little Collins St.,
Melbourne + 9662 1026

3 The Tote
Iconic Melbourne rock pub named after the illegal betting shops that once dotted the area.
71 Johnston St.,
Melbourne + 9419 5320

4 Albert's Basement/Catfood Press
Albert's Basement is a collective of Melbourne music lovers who organize several gigs a month in warehouses and bedrooms. Catfood is one such space.
289 Lygon St.,
Melbourne (no phone)

5 Irene Community Arts Warehouse
A former lingerie factory, now a collectively run non-profit venue with an activist sensibility. Hosts shows of punk, hardcore, grindcore, and other loud genres favored by straight-edgers.
5 Pitt St.,
Melbourne + 9387 9699

6 Missing Link Records
405 Bourke St.,
Melbourne + 9670 8208

7 Polyester Records Store - 1
288 Flinders Lane,
Melbourne + 9663 8696

8 Polyester Records Store - 2
387 Brunswick St.,
Melbourne + 9419 5137

9 Louie's Warehouse
Warehouse gigs are a more recent development in Sydney, but this one, in the inner-west suburb of Marrickville, is pretty popular.
34 Murray St.,
Sydney (no phone)

10 Red Eye Records Store - New/Imports
66 King St.,
Sydney + 9299 4233

11 Red Eye Records Store - Second Hand
370 Pitt St.,
Sydney + 9262 8755

12 Ric's Bar, Fatboys Cafe
Located in Fortitude Valley, once Brisbane's red-light district. Now it's a live music hub. Downstairs at Fatboy's, you'll find pizza, burgers, and fried breakfasts.
321 Brunswick St.,
Brisbane + 1800 084 418

13 Rocking Horse Records
245 Albert St.,
Brisbane + 3229 5360

14 78 Records
914 Hay St.,
Perth + 9322 6384

Zoc
Go

Royc

Flemington Rd **PARK**

**NORTH
MELBOURN**

DOCKLAN

**WORLD TR
CENTRE**

West Gate Fw

11: THE DIGITAL DOMAIN

by Eve Hyman

17th-18th c.
Cumbe (clave + drum music) brought to South America by Guinean slaves.

1920s
Bands elevate cumbia to level of dance hall music.

1960s
Peru adopts cumbia, adds surf guitar, and calls it chicha.

1980s-1990s
Synthesizers "kidnap" cumbia from all folk music history. Argentina's economic collapse gives birth to cumbia villera.

2000s
First experimental cumbia festival, Festicumex, takes place. "New cumbia" begins to spread throughout Buenos Aires, and eventually, to the world at large.

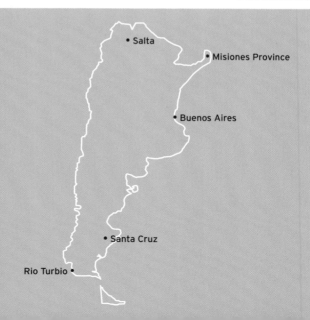

- Salta
- Misiones Province
- Buenos Aires
- Santa Cruz
- Rio Turbio

ARGENTINA : THE DIGITAL DOMAIN

Congreso Nacional and monument photo ©Merrry Photography

Buenos Aires (San Telmo) photo ©Gustavo Minas

Puerto Madero photo ©subman

Kumbia Queers photo ©Kumbia Queers

Buenos Aires is synonymous with tango, yet cumbia is what more Argentines dance to. Cumbia's signature accordion-as-bass-line is found throughout Mexico, down through Panama, and across the borders of Colombia, Peru, and Bolivia.

Also known as tropicál, it's the sound of small towns and working-class neighborhoods, and it serves to connect Euro-intoxicated Buenos Aires to the rest of Latin America. In the South American capital, cumbia spills out of passing cars, dominates suburban nightclubs, and provides the soundtrack for dancing the day away at Sunday barbeques.

Cumbia may well be the most widespread of Latin rhythms, and it has been making its way up to Europe and North America of late. Like many American continental rhythms, it's a blend of the old and new worlds, with roots in Africa, but unlike traditions such as salsa or calypso, it has wound its way on a vast, nomadic journey throughout

BEFORE YOU GO, GET IN THE KNOW

Websites:

www.lacongona.com

www.mondomix.com

www.maddecent.com/blog

www.duttyartz.com

www.lafamilydub.blogspot.com

www.negrophonic.com

Magazines:

Time Out Buenos Aires

Urb

The Fader

XLR8R

Pablo Lescano of Damas Gratis
The godfather of urban cumbia. Lescano started cumbia villera in the late 90s and continues to innovate and keep it vibrant with constant touring, media appearances, and his demi-god persona.
photo: ©La Yumba

El Hijo de la Cumbia
Makes most blogged-about Buenos Aires exports, merging Colombian, Mexican, and Argentine cumbia with reggae and hip-hop influences that add up to highly danceable tracks with wide appeal.
photo: ©Emiliano Gomez

Dick el Demasiado
Began the experimental cumbia movement when he concocted a fictional music festival during a cinematic romp through Honduras.
photo: ©Patwasi Pat Taylor

Kumbia Queers
Your new favorite lesbian band with the cumbia cover of Madonna's "La Isla Bonita" and a metal ditty that begins with a Black Sabbath guitar riff.
photo: ©Kumbia Queers

Villa Diamante
Brought mash-ups to cumbia, introducing Lil' Wayne to Los Palmeras and blending MIA over Calle 13 and traditional Colombian cumbia. He is the gateway cumbia DJ, making the music accessible to people who've never purchased music with Spanish lyrics.
photo: ©Mar Van der Aa

Chancha via Circuito
Breathes new art into Andean music. With cumbia as a reference point, his tracks hold percussion tracks up to the light and splice traditional drums with machete sounds, indigenous chants, and minimal electronic bleeps and sighs.
photo: ©Chancha Via Circuito

ALBUMS THAT INFLUENCE CUMBIA IN BUENOS AIRES

Damas Gratis
Para los Pibes (For the Kids) (2000)

El Hijo de la Cumbia
Freestyle de Ritmos (Rhythm Freestyle) (2008)

Various Artists
The Roots of Chicha: Psychedelic Cumbias from Peru (2007)

Los Angeles Azules
Inolvidables (Unforgettables) (1996)

Zizek
ZZK Sound Vol. 2 (2009)

Los Palmeras
Un Sentimiento (A Feeling) (2004)

Bomba Estereo
Estalla (Burst) (2008)

Andres Landero
16 Canciones de Andres Landero (16 Songs by Andres Landero) (1997)

Toy Hernandez
The Mexmore (2009)

Petrona Martinez
Bonito que Canta (How Lovely S/he Sings) (2002)

South and Central America, making it a musical chameleon. Only the blues has morphed as much; cumbia is associated with a spectrum of sounds that appeal to fans of everything from country ballads to gangster rap. But while cumbia is a pan-American sound practiced by legendary artists out of Colombia, Mexico, and Peru, mention it to a middle-class Argentine and you'll get a frown. The genre is considered low-class and unsophisticated by many in this most proudly European of South American nations. Nonetheless, Buenos Aires has become the center of the latest incarnation of cumbia, adding electronic influences to the rural sound, launching it to premier music festivals overseas, and connecting a new audience to Latin music.

Cumbia's first documented appearance was on Colombia's northern coast in the early 19th century, where it was used in the struggle for independence from Spain; but it probably dates back another one-to-two-hundred years to when cumbe, a West African clave and drum form, was brought over by slaves from Guinea. The drums were layered in with the wind and string instruments played by natives to create music that became associated with a courtship ritual. The new genre symbolized the union between the Africans

and indigenous Colombians, as well as their solidarity against Spanish oppressors. One cumbia creation myth tells the story of natives and slaves finding accordions washed up on the beach after a German shipwreck, explaining how a central European instrument became the signature sound in a cultural melange.

In the 1920s, big bands took on cumbia and elevated it to the dance hall, where it shrugged off its folk music past and became South American pop. Cumbia made its way to New York City by the 30s, where Puerto Rican immigrants filled in for the too-big-to-ship Colombian orchestra, and radio helped it spread across Mexico, where regional Native American influences were added and Mexican cumbia took on a life of its own. By the 1960s, Peru had adopted cumbia and added surf guitars, calling it chicha, and some of cumbia's classics emerged. Peru's Los Mirlos recorded the cumbia classic, "Cumbia de los Pajaritos," and later Bolivia produced a cumbia record that went platinum. Los Palmeras, from the northern province of Santa Fe in Argentina, were the pop cumbia band of the 70s, and spread the Santefesino sound throughout the country.

⌃ **El Hijo De La Cumbia** photo: ©Evan Browning

The weekly party of Zizek Club, which led to the creation of the label ZZK Records, is an
artists' collective that serves to facilitate innovative dance sounds—with an emphasis on

BUILDING YOUR OWN COLLECTION

Any record store in downtown Buenos Aires will carry cumbia, though the broadest selection is to be found in the small stores all around Constitución train station. In the interest of personal safety, satisfying cumbia purchases can easily be made at Miles – Honduras 4912 or at Zivals – Serrano 1445, both located in Palermo Soho.

Offsite, Turntable Lab in NYC's East Village gives access to the latest in hipster cumbia with releases from ZZK and Bersa Records. The Latin music hub of Brooklyn's Sunset Park allows for ample cumbia exploration, along 4th and 5th Avenues from the mid 30s to 60th street.

On the west coast of the U.S., the Hollywood location of Amoeba Records is a proud proponent of cumbia while independent stores like Julio's in San Francisco's Mission cater to Spanish language releases. A trip to Sunset Junction through Silverlake and Echo Park via Sunset Boulevard (also in LA) turns up a number of mom-and-pop shops as well, with vintage Latin records including cumbia from Colombia and Mexico.

Inside Amoeba Records photo: ©Dave Miller

In the 80s and 90s, synthesized keyboards and reverb-heavy romantic ballads kidnapped cumbia, stripping it of any semblance of its folk roots. When the banks went insolvent and economic crisis gripped Argentina, cumbia villera reared its head with violent, misogynist lyrics celebrating drug abuse and glorifying the nihilist, crime-ridden world of the new shantytowns (or villas miseries). Always marginalized in Argentina, cumbia now had the promotion of violence and crime added to its list of sins by critics with the emergence of Damas Gratis's gangster-rap take on the form. Argentine cumbia villera joined American rap and Mexican

corridos as an urban art form expressing the reality of an economically depressed community. It later spawned an intellectual counterpoint with 2003's experimental cumbia that includes elements of global dance music and is both optimistic and musically informed.

The bailanta is cumbia's juke joint, the neighborhood dance hall where locals gather to hear live bands and dance the night away. There are only two bailantas in the capital city of Buenos Aires. Most live shows are relegated to warehouse-size clubs outside city limits, which host live bands on the tour circuit to packed houses of young fans. In the past few years, DJs and performers of new cumbia have begun playing at popular nightclubs throughout Buenos Aires—boliches that operate outside the traditional bailanta network.

Festicumex, an international cumbia and electronic-music festival, was held in 2003 in Buenos Aires and spawned "experimental cumbia." Beginning as an artistic whim of eccentric cumbia artist Dick El Demasiado, it inspired local musicians and visiting Europeans of all stripes to try their hand at cumbia, and a movement was born. Kumbia Queers, ZZK Records, Bersa Records, and Señor Coconut all followed Dick's lead, and though the festival only came together once more, today their legacy lives on with weekly parties, live shows, and recordings of electro-cumbia in bars, cafes, and irregular venues around the city.

The sepia-toned image of tango may thrive on the elite dance circuit in Buenos Aires, and in the popular conception of this elegant, enigmatic city, but the new music catching on here—and around the world—is local cumbia. From velvet-rope clubs to parked cars on questionable corners, cumbia is the ever present heartbeat of Buenos Aires. Steady and haunting, its rhythm fits the pace of life in the Paris of the South, translating some of its secrets through song.

Emiliano Gomez (El Hijo de la Cumbia) also contributed to this article as a consultant to the writer.

︿ **Festicumex** photo:©Maria Isabel Rueda
‹ **La Boca landmark, Caminito** photo: ©Frank K.

ZZK Club photo: © ZZK Records

MAP OF VENUES
AND CITY LANDMARKS

1 Voodoo Motel
Hosts weekly Zizek parties on Thursdays, bringing out the best in new cumbia.
1735 Av Dorrego
+ 3546 3480

2 Plaza Serrano
Located on the other side of Palermo. Turns its restaurants into nightclubs late on the weekends.
The intersection of Calle Serrano and Honduras.

3 Moliere
Located in historic San Telmo. Plays cumbia along with popular music of every variant.
299 Chile
+ 4343 2623

4 Fugees 99
Not far from Moliere. Plays cumbia villera alongside hip-hop and reggaeton.
1190 Bolívar
info@fugees.com.ar

5 Rumi
An elegant, large space reserved for electronica most nights, except Fridays when Latin music reigns.
Figueroa Alcorta 6442
y La Pampa
+ 4782 1398

6 Niceto
Home to live shows by the Kumbia Queers, Dick El Demasiado, and Pablo Lescano alike. Supported new cumbia from its inception.
5510 Av Cnel. Niceto Vega
+ 4779 9396

7 Luna Park
Legendary venue where Evita met Perón at a formal dance. Now the setting for collaborations between cumbia legends and bands and guests from the rock and reggaeton worlds.
420 Av. Madero
+ 5279 5279

8 Fantastico
An authentic bailanta.
3475 Av. Rivadavia
(no phone)

9 Constitución Railway Station
Large railway terminal in the heart of Buenos Aires.
Avenida General Hornos 11
at Plaza Constitución
+ 4304 0023

10 Palermo Soho
An area in the northeast part of the city. Home to great art, culture, and nightlife.

photo: ©Ed Vill

Av Leopoldo Lugones

Figueroa Alcorta

**AEROPARQUE
JORGE NEWBERY**

Del Libertador

. Justo

Pte. Arturo Illia

Av Tomas A. Edison

10

Raul Scalabrini Ortiz

**CAPILLA CRISTO
OBRERO**

RECOLETA

Av Cordoba

Av Corrientes

Au. 9 de Mayo

7

**BUENOS
AIRES**

Av Paseo Colon

Av Entre Rios

AGRO

8

Av Rivadavia

Av Jujuy

3

Au. 9 de Mayo

Av Independencia

Castro Barros

Av San Juan

4

Au. 25 de Mayo

CONSTITUCION

9

181

Au. 25 de Mayo

12: FOLK LURE

by Jessica Hundley

1930s ▶▶▶

Dust Bowl forces mass exodus to California and brings with it Calicountry music. Roy Rogers forms the Sons of Pioneers, one of the first commercial bands of the genre.

1960–1970s ▶▶▶

Calicountry is infused with grit, and sends its roots outward to outlaw lands. Gram Parsons dies; Merle Haggard keeps on keepin' on. The Eagles become the genre's biggest act of all time.

1980s ▶▶▶

Calicountry is thrown into the shadow of Sunset Strip Hair Metal madness, but alt-punk acts like X keep the honky-tonk dream alive.

1990s-2000s

Dwight Yoakam takes the reigns. Alt-country acts like Wilco spread the word to the masses. Calicountry, alt country, and folk all experience an indie rock renaissance.

Bakersfield

Topanga Canyon

Pioneertown

Laurel Canyon

Joshua Tree

Los Angeles

Indio

Topanga Canyon photo: @ndebts

Roy Rogers and Dale Evans
photo: ©Alan Light

Topanga Canyon
photo:©Matthew Robinson

Bakersfield Arch at Buck Owen's
Palace photo:© David Geohring

BAKERSFIELD

Websites:

www.laweekly.com

www.LA.com

www.larecord.com

www.arthurmag.com

www.losanjealous.com

www.whenyouawake.com

www.aquariumdrunkard.com

www.halcyon-magazine.com

Magazines:

Flaunt

Anthem

Calicountry, the dust-blown cowboy strut that began with the Okie folk songs of the Dust Bowl émigrés, continues to hang over Los Angeles like campfire smoke. This is American country music refined by the long haul West, when the call of Manifest Destiny lured Depression-era farmers to take their rusted trucks way out to California—the land of rich soil and everlasting sunshine.

It's the rough and tumble, hard-scrabble sound of sweat and dirt colliding with the glitz and glamour of the Hollywood Singing Cowboys, the early stars of the small and silver screens who rode into the sunset with a long song on their lips. California is the last and final stop for roots and Americana music, and Calicountry—ever-evolving—reflects the starry-eyed dreaming, free-love rambling, and blown-out yellow sky of the Golden State itself.

The sound's undisputed epicenter is Los Angeles. The city, with its low-lying haze of lost dreams and

> **Roy Rogers and his horse Trigger** photo:©The Roy Rogers-Dale Evans Museum in Branson, MO

Roy Rogers

Formed the Western music group Sons of the Pioneers in 1934 and went on to release such cowboy classics as "Tumbling Tumbleweeds."

photo: ©:The Roy Rogers-Dale Evans Museum in Branson, MO

Gene Autry

Immortalized Western roots in Los Angeles with the founding of the Gene Autry Western Heritage Museum, which houses much of Autry's own collection of Western art and Hollywood cowboy memorabilia.

photo: ©Tom Lohdan

Buck Owens

The patron saint of Calicountry, a pioneering voice who, along with his legendary band, the Buckaroos, created a fascinating hybrid that he dubbed American Music. photo: ©Buck Owens Productions Co., Inc.

Merle Haggard
One of the most popular proponents of Calicountry, recording much of his catalogue in Los Angeles and at his home studio up the freeway in Bakersfield.
photo: ©Travis Lide

Gram Parsons
Founder of The Flying Burrito Brothers and a member of The Byrds, he also discovered Emmylou Harris, with whom he made two albums before his death as a result of a drug overdose in 1973.

SEE IT FOR YOURSELF

photo: ©Jeff Owens

Stagecoach (Indio, CA)
An annual jamboree in April put together by the creators of Coachella. Stagecoach is one of the largest country music festivals in the nation. Held each year just a few hours outside of town, it brings together both big-name contemporary acts and living legends.

ALBUMS THAT INFLUENCED CALICOUNTRY IN THE LA AREA

Gram Parsons
Grievous Angel
(1974)

The Byrds
Sweetheart of the Rodeo (1968)

Merle Haggard
Mama Tried (1968)

CSNY
Déjà Vu (1970)

Buffalo Springfield
Self-Titled (1966)

Gene Clark
Live at Ebbets Field (1975)
Lee Hazlewood
Trouble is a Lonesome Town (1963)
Emmylou Harris
Pieces of the Sky (1975)
The Flying Burrito Brothers
The Gilded Palace of Sin (1972)
Buck Owens
The Fabulous Country Music Sound of Buck Owens (1962)

wandering angels, is a locale particularly suited to the making of lonely, heart-achy music. Search around its craggy canyons and cavernous studios and you'll find a long, rich history of Calicountry wonders.

From its humble origins, Calicountry music has grown from its first raw forms into something much more, like a tumbleweed gaining size as it rolls, ever onward. With the turmoil, decadence, and inner-expansion of the 60s, the sound put down new roots in outlaw lands, taking on the silky sheen of rock 'n' roll excess and the tough grit of electric guitars.

The musicians grew their hair long

^ [top] **Amoeba Music** photo: ©Daquella Manera
[bottom] **Gene Autry Museum** photo: ©David Hoshor

and mixed Hollywood flash with dirty denim. The lyrics moved from squeaky clean tales of cowboy heroics into poetic odes to hard drugs and pretty women.

Calicountry has been continually redefined and resurrected ever since, to emerge as an all-encompassing sound—a multi-quilted blend of everything from folksy dreaming to ghost town haunt to raucous, beer-buzz sway. But always, the mountain/desert/ocean freedom of California is its inspiration.

The Calicountry scene is still going strong. If you head down to Molly Malone's on Fairfax in LA, you can hear the uptempo rock-inflected twang of local acts like Mike Stinson, Dave Gleason, or I See Hawks in LA. Check out Amoeba Records on Sunset for some of the best selection of Calicountry up-and-comers.

You can also find some of the best local and national Calicountry acts playing out in the desert at spots like the secluded Palms Bar in Twentynine Palms or the Joshua Tree's finest BBQ joint/honky-tonk Pappy and Harriet's Pioneertown Palace. The house band at this latter High Desert hideaway is an incredible collection of seasoned studio musicians dubbed, The Thriftstore Allstars. Come on Sundays and you might see them backing anyone from Lucinda Williams to Dwight Yoakam.

^ **Los Angeles** photo: ©Todd Jones Photography

SIDE ROADS AND SISTER CITIES

Bakersfield

Positioned at the southern end of the San Joaquin Valley, Bakersfield served for generations as a home base for Texas immigrants heading west. It's that Texan twang, along with bright Telecaster and pedal steel guitar, which serves as the foundation for what is known as the "Bakersfield Sound."

Joshua Tree

During the 60s and 70s, the desert landscape of Joshua Tree was a muse for a new breed of psychedelic country music; everyone from the Rolling Stones to Gram Parsons made the trek from Los Angeles in search of hallucinogenic inspiration. After his death, Parsons's body was absconded by a roadie and burned in Joshua Tree National Park, making the area a mandatory stop on any Calicountry pilgrimage.

Pioneertown

A former Western movie set, Pioneertown has been transformed into a fully functioning burg about 130 miles east of the real Hollywood. The town's one road (Mane Street) offers a few hundred yards of dirt-trail lined with ramshackle Old West storefronts and a few weatherworn saloons, among them the popular Pappy and Harriet's.

photo: ©Clinton Steeds

Topanga Canyon and Laurel Canyon

These two neighborhoods were home to many freewheeling folk- and country-rock musicians during the 60s and 70s, including Neil Young, Joni Mitchell, and members of The Byrds.

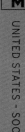

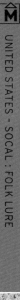

Cholla Cactus Garden, Joshua Tree National Park photo ©Eric Foltz Photography

CALICOUNTRY TODAY

The Calicountry stars of the past have had a huge influence on its present day practitioners. They laid a complex groundwork of sounds that has helped shape the category. Here's a roundup of a few current and up-and-coming artists worth checking out.

Jenny Lewis

Much has been made of Jenny Lewis's first band, Rilo Kiley, but this LA-based, singer-songwriter's current solo work is just as exciting. Weaving the genres of folk, country, and Southern gospel together, and citing influences everywhere from Joni Mitchell to Gram Parsons to Barbra Streisand, *Jenny Lewis's Rabbit Fur Coat* (2006) and *Acid Tongue* (2008) are records full of maturity and wit.

⌃ **Los Angeles** at twilight photo: ©S. Greg Panosian

The Watson Twins

Honing their vocal chops in their church choir in their hometown of Louisville, KY, The Watson Twins emigrated to LA and immediately became an essential element within the fertile Silverlake indie folk/country scene, collaborating with the likes of Jenny Lewis and playing their unique double trouble folk harmonies to audiences around the world. The duo scored a hit with a dreamy, lilting cover of The Cure's "Just Like Heaven," and continue to lull audiences into blissful oblivion with their popular live performances.

Vetiver

San Francisco's Vetiver is quite possibly one of the most talented bands around, mainly due in part to the incredible song writing/vocal magic of band leader Andy Cabic. His gorgeous, layered folk, haunting country-inflected ballads, and ghostly, seductive music feed the soul.

Fruit Bats

A newly baptized Angeleno, Eric D. Johnson has played with everyone from Vetiver to The Shins, but his own Fruit Bats is where he experiments with honky-tonk stomp and dreamy country rock. This is a talented multi-instrumentalist who stretches his wings and flies over favored lands—think early Fleetwood Mac, Neil Young, and other Laurel Canyon stalwarts, morphed into something wholly new.

Mike Stinson

The undisputed king of the LA country scene, Mike Stinson has been rocking the local (and national) stages with his unique take on the genre. Usually backed by some of the finest country-lovin' musicians in the state, Stinson puts together a high-energy honky-tonk romp reminiscent of the Sunset Strip's Golden Era of The Byrds and The Flying Burrito Brothers.

Devendra Banhart

Combining folk, Brasilia, rock 'n' roll weirdness and the occasional country romp, Angeleno/child of the world, Banhart is a kind of modern-day mystic chameleon. His albums veer across a broad range of inspirations, from Laurel Canyon sunny day folk to South American samba. A shaman and jester, prophet and poet, Banhart just might be the merriest prankster of the neo-folk scene.

She & Him

A musical group formed by Zooey Deschanel and M. Ward, She & Him merge traditional folk melodies with choir-like harmonies, creating a new type of music rooted in folk and country.

∧ [top] **Jenny Lewis** photo: ©J Caldwell
[bottom] **Devendra Banhart** photo: ©Ella Mullins

MAP OF VENUES AND CITY LANDMARKS

1 Gene Autry Museum Of Western Heritage
Rotating art exhibits and an annual summer barbecue-and-concert series make this a must-see for anyone interested in Calicountry's historical roots.
4700 Western Heritage Way, LA + 323 667 2000

2 Chateau Marmont
Notorious hotel, built in 1927, that hosted a slew of Hollywood troublemakers over the years. The setting for a lot of music lore (Led Zeppelin once road motorcycles through the lobby).
8221 W. Sunset Blvd., West Hollywood + 323 656 1010

3 Laurel Canyon
A nexus of counterculture activity and attitudes in the 60s. Home to many of LA's top rock musicians, such as Frank Zappa and The Byrds.
Located between West Hollywood and the San Fernando Valley

4 The Troubadour
Seminal rock 'n' roll venue, arguably Hollywood's most famous nightclub. Fostered a new direction for Calicountry in the 60s.
9081 Santa Monica Blvd., West Hollywood + 310 276 6168

5 El Cid/Ronnie Mack's Barn Dance
Classic country event that takes place here the first Tuesday of each month.
4212 Sunset Blvd., LA + 323 668 0318

6 Grand Ole Echo
A thriving rock venue that offers up a daytime roots-and-Americana jam, complete with delicious barbecue every Sunday in the summer.
1822 W. Sunset Blvd., LA + 213 413 8200

7 Topanga Canyon
Home to many freewheeling folk- and country-rock musicians during the 60s and 70s.
Located in the Santa Monica Mountains

8 Buck Owens' Crystal Palace
A renown showcase for a slew of country greats.
2800 Buck Owens Blvd., Bakersfield + 661 328 7560

9 The Stagecoach Festivals
One of the largest country music festivals in the nation. Features big-name contemporary acts and living legends.
Empire Polo Club 81-800 Avenue 51 Indio + 760 342 2762

10 Pappy And Harriet's
The self-proclaimed "best honky tonk West of the Mississippi." Features live acts from LA and beyond, focusing on country, roots, and Americana.
53688 Pioneertown Rd, Pioneertown + 760 365 5956

11 Pioneertown
A former Western movie set, transformed into a fully functioning burg about 130 miles east of the real Hollywood.
Located in the Morongo Basin region, near San Bernardino

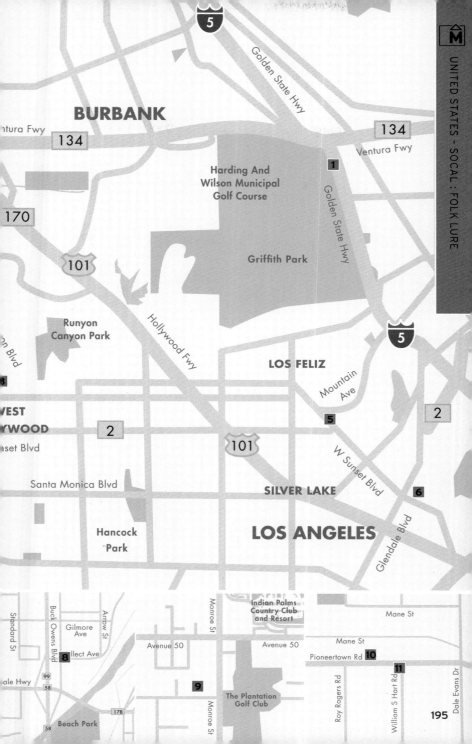

BURBANK

134

Ventura Fwy

134

Ventura Fwy

170

101

Harding And
Wilson Municipal
Golf Course

Griffith Park

Runyon
Canyon Park

Hollywood Fwy

LOS FELIZ

Mountain
Ave

WEST
YWOOD

2

101

SILVER LAKE

Santa Monica Blvd

Hancock
Park

LOS ANGELES

W Sunset Blvd

Glendale Blvd

Golden State Hwy

Golden State Hwy

Standard St

Buck Owens Blvd

Gilmore
Ave

Arrow St

llect Ave

ale Hwy

99

58

Beach Park

178

58

Avenue 50

Monroe St

Monroe St

Indian Palms
Country Club
and Resort

Avenue 50

The Plantation
Golf Club

Mane St

Mane St

Pioneertown Rd

Roy Rogers Rd

William S Hart Rd

Dale Evans Dr

INDEX+CREDITS
DISCOGRAPHY

ARTIST	ALBUM	YEAR
10	Nomad	2008
Abd al Malik	Le Face à Face des Cœurs (Hearts Face to Face)	2004
Akhenaton	Métèque et Mat (Checkmate)	1999
Aleks and the Ramps	Pisces vs. Aquarius	2007
Aleksandr Novikov	Vezi Menya Izvozchik (Let's Go Cabman!)	*
Ali	Chaos et Harmonie (Chaos and Harmony)	2005
Ananda Shankar	Remembering	2008
Andres Landero	16 Canciones de (16 Songs by) Andres Landero	1997
Anthony Braxton	3 Compositions of New Jazz	1968
AR Rahman	Vande Mataram	1997
Arkady Severny i Ansambl Elita	Nochnoy Taxi (Night Taxi)	*
Arkady Severny	Fartovy Yad (Lucky Poison)	*
Arkady Severny	Koloda Kart (Deck of Cards)	*
Art Ensemble of Chicago	Americans Swinging in Paris: The Pathe Sessions	1969–70
Aster Aweke	Aster	1989
Beijing New Music Ensemble	Wild Grass	2009
Blood or Whiskey	Cashed Out on Culture	2005
Blood or Whiskey	Self-Titled	1996
Bole 2 Harlem	Bole 2 Harlem, Vol. 1	2006
Bomba Estereo	Estalla (Burst)	2008
Booka Shade	Movements	2006
Bratya Zhemchuzhnye	Mamashi Spyat (Mama's Sleep)	*
Buck Owens	The Fabulous Country Music Sound of Buck Owens	1962
Buffalo Springfield	Self-Titled	1966
Bülent Arel (and various artists)	Pioneers of Electronic Music	2006
Carsick Cars	Self-Titled	2007
Cihat Aşkın	Istanbulin	2007
Colourblind	Self-Titled	2008
CSNY	Déjà Vu	1970
Daler Mehndi	Bolo Ta Ra Ra	1995
Damas Gratis	Para Los Pibes (For the Kids)	2000
Derrick Carter & Mark Farina	Live at OM	2004
Dina Vierny	Chants du Goulag (Songs of the Gulag)	*
Earl "Fatha" Hines	Earl Hines and the Duke's Men	1944–47

ARTIST	ALBUM	YEAR
El Hijo de la Cumbia	Freestyle de Ritmos (Rhythm Freestyle)	2008
Ellen Allien	Berlinette	2003
Emmylou Harris	Pieces of the Sky	1975
Emre Aracı	Sultan Portreleri and "Bosphorus in Moonlight" Violin Concerto	1997
Erdem Helvacioğlu	Altered Realities	2007
Essendon Airport	Sonic Investigations of the Trivial	2002
Euphoria	Dhoom	1998
Fabe	Befa Surprend Ses Frères (Befa Surprises His Brothers)	1995
Fabulous Diamonds	7 Songs	2008
Fazıl Say	Silk Road (and other works)	1994
Flogging Molly	Drunken Lullabies	2002
FM3	The Buddha Machine (not actually an album, but a music box)	2008
Fred Anderson & Hamid Drake	From the River to the Ocean	2007
Garik Sukachev i Aleksandr Sklyar	Botsman i Brodyaga (A Boatswain and a Tramp)	*
Gary Lawyer	The Other Side of Dawn	1993
Gene Ammons	The Gene Ammons Story: Gentle Jug	1961-63
Gene Clark	Live at Ebbets Field	1975
Gigi	Gold and Wax	2006
Gram Parsons	Grievous Angel	1974
Gui Boratto	Chromophobia	2007
Hand Hell	Phonography	2007
Henrik Schwarz	Henrik Schwarz Live	2007
IAM	L'École du Micro d'Argent (The School of the Silver Mic)	1997
Idil Biret	Brahms: Complete Piano Works	2001
Idil Biret	Rachmaninov: Piano Concertos 2 & 3	1998
Kamran Ince	Symphony No. 3, No. 4, "Domes"/Prague Symphony Orchestra	2005
Keny Arkana	Entre Ciment et Belle Étoile (Between Cement and Beautiful Stars)	2006
Kes Band	The Grey Goose Wing	2007
Kraftwerk	Computer World	1981
Lee Hazlewood	Trouble is a Lonesome Town	1963
Lesopoval	Ya Kuplyu Tebe Dom (I Will Buy You a House)	*
Leyla Gencer	Bellini: "Beatrice di Tenda"	1964

ARTIST	ALBUM	YEAR
Leyla Gencer	Bellini: "Norma"	1964
Li Jianhong	Bird	2007
Los Angeles Azules	Inolvidables (Unforgettable)	1996
Los Palmeras	Un Sentimiento (A Feeling)	2004
Louis Armstrong	The Complete Hot Five and Hot Seven Recordings	1925–28
Louiz Banks	Miles From India	2008
Mahmoud Ahmed	Yitbarek	2003
MBS	Le Micro Brise le Silence (The Mic Breaks the Silence)	2002
Médine	11 Septembre, Récit du 11ème Jour (September 11, or the Narrative of the Same Day)	2004
Merle Haggard	Mama Tried	1968
Miquia	Sign Language	2005
Modeselektor	Happy Birthday!	2007
Muluken Melesse	Muluken Melesse, Vol. 1	2008
Nicole Mitchell's Black Earth Ensemble	Black Unstoppable	2007
Paranoid Visions	40 Shades of Gangreen	2007
Pentagram	It's OK, It's All Good	2007
Petrona Martinez	Bonito Que Canta (How Lovely S/he Sings)	2002
Primitive Calculators et al	Primitive Calculators and Friends	2007
Rabbi	Self-Titled	2004
Raghu Dixit Project	Self-Titled	1998
Rahel Yohannes	Menelik	2003
Ricardo Villalobos	Fabric 36	2007
Richie Hawtin	DE9: Closer to the Edit	2001
Shaa'ir + Func	Light Tribe	2008
Shankar-Ehsaan-Loy	Soundtrack: Dil Chahta Hai	2001
Shewandagn Hailu	SK Alegn	2004
Shubha Mudgal	Ab Ke Sawan	2001
Sinik	Sang Froid (Cold Blood)	2006
Sun Ra	Jazz in Silhouette	1958
Teddy Afro	Yasteseryal	2005
The Birthday Party/Boys Next Door	The Birthday Party	1980
The Byrds	Sweetheart of the Rodeo	1968
The Dropkick Murphys	Sing Loud, Sing Proud	2001

ARTIST	ALBUM	YEAR
The Dubliners	Seven Drunken Nights	1967
The Flying Burrito Brothers	The Gilded Palace of Sin	1972
The Go-Betweens	Liberty Belle and the Black Diamond Express	1986
The Pogues	If I Should Fall From Grace with God	1987
The Pogues	Rum, Sodomy & the Lash	1985
The Saints	(I'm) Stranded	1977
The Skids	Scared to Dance	1979
Thin Lizzy	Jailbreak	1976
Tilahun Gessesse	Greatest Hits	2000
Toy Hernandez	The Mexmore	2009
Trofim	Aristokratija: Pomoyki (Gutter Aristocracy)	*
True Radical Miracle	Cockroaches	2006
Usha Uthup	Soundtrack: Shaan	1980
Vandermark 5	Beat Reader	2008
Various Artists (compiled by Yan Jun)	Noise is Free	2008
Various Artists	Morts Pour Rien (Dead for Nothing)	2007
Various Artists	The Roots of Chicha: Psychadelic Cumbias from Peru	2007
Various Artists	The Very Best of Ethiopiques	2007
Various Artists	Tresor Mix, Vol. 1-5	2007-08
Villi Tokarev	V Shomnom Balagane (In a Noisy Sideshow)	*
Vladimir Vysotsky	Kupola (Domes)	*
Vladimir Vysotsky	Rechechka (Tiny River)	*
Vladimir Vysotsky	Tatuirovka (Tattoo)	*
Von Freeman	The Improvisor	2002
Wang Fan	Sound of Meditation Within the Body	2001
White	Self-Titled	2008
Xiao He	2009 Europe Tour	TBD
Zizek	ZZK Sound Vol. 2	2009

(*NOTE: There are no specific release dates for these albums since originally many of these recordings circulated hand-to-hand as samizdat and were not packaged and sold as albums.)

FESTIVALS

APPENDIX

FESTIVAL	GENRE	MONTH
Australia		
Applecore (Melbourne)	Art Rock	Feb
Big Day Out (Across Australia and New Zealand)	Rock/Hip-Hop/Electronic	Jan-Feb
Cherry Rock (Melbourne)	Art Rock	Apr
Global Gathering (Across Australia)	Electronic	Nov
Golden Plains (Victoria)	Art Rock	Mar
Meredith Music Festival (Victoria)	Art Rock	Dec
Parklife (Across Australia–Brisbane, Perth, Melbourne, Sydney, Adelaide)	Multi-Genre	Sep-Oct
Spring/Summer/Autumn/Winter Tones (Throughout Australia)	Art Rock	Seasonal
St. Jerome's Laneway (Across Australia)	Art Rock	Feb-Mar
We Love Sounds (Across Australia)	Techno	Jun
Austria		
Snowbombing (Mayrhofen)	Electronic	Mar–Apr
Belgium		
I Love Techno (Gent)	Techno	Oct
Rock Werchter (Werchter)	Rock	Jul
Burkina Faso		
FESPACO (Burkina Faso)	Pan-African Film + Music	Mar
China		
Fun Fair Festival (Beijing)	Multi-Genre	May
Intro (Beijing)	Electronic/Experimental	May
Midi Modern Music Festival (Beijing)	Multi-Genre	May
Mini Midi Festival (Beijing)	Multi-Genre	May
Strawberry Music Festival (Beijing)	Multi-Genre	May
Zebra Music Festival (Chengdu)	Multi-Genre	May
Colombia		
Rock Al Parque (Bogotá)	Rock	Jun
Denmark		
Roskilde Festival (Roskilde)	Multi-Genre	Jul
Germany		
Popkomm (Berlin, Germany)	Multi-Genre	Summer
Iceland		
Iceland Airwaves (Reykjavik)	Multi-Genre	Oct
India		
Congo Square Jazz Fest (Kolkata)	Jazz	Jan-Feb
Eastwind (New Delhi)	Multi-Genre	Feb
Independence Rock Festival (Mumbai)	Rock	Aug-Sep
Jazz Utsav (Mumbai/Delhi)	Jazz	Nov
Joydeb Mela (West Bengal)	Multi-Genre	Jan
One Tree Festival (Mumbai)	Multi-Genre	Feb

FESTIVAL	GENRE	MONTH
India (cont'd)		
Pous Mela (Kolkata)	Indipop	Dec
Rajasthan International Folk Festival (Rajasthan)	Folk	Oct
Rock in India (Bangalore)	Metal	Mar
Roots Festival (Northeast India)	Multi-Genre	Spring
Sunburn Festival (Goa)	Electronic	Dec
Ireland		
Oxegen (County Kildare)	Rock/Pop	Jul
Temple Bar TradFest (Dublin)	Multi-Genre	Jan-Feb
Japan		
Fuji Rock (Naeba)	Rock	Jul
Summer Sonic (Tokyo & Osaka)	Rock/Alternative/Pop	Aug
Jamaica		
Reggae Sumfest (Montego Bay)	Reggae/R&B/Hip-Hop	Jul
Malaysia		
Rainforest World Music Festival (Borneo)	World Music	Jul
Netherlands		
Pinkpop (Landgraaf)	Rock	May-Jun
Norway		
Oya Festival (Oslo)	Rock/Indie/Electronic	Aug
Russia		
Chanson of the Year Awards Show (Moscow)	Chanson	Mar
Serbia		
EXIT (Novi Sad)	Techno/Rock/Hip-Hop	Jul
Spain		
Benicassim (Benicassim)	Rock/Pop/Electronic	Jul
Ibiza Rocks (Ibiza)	Multi-Genre	Sep
Monegros Desert Festival (Fraga)	Techno	Jul
Primavera Sound (Barcelona)	Multi-Genre	May-Jun
Sonar (Barcelona)	Electronic	Jun-Sep
Switzerland		
Guinness Irish Festival (Sion)	Irish	Aug
Turkey		
Akbank Guitar Festival (Istanbul)	Classical	Mar
IKSV Klasik Müzik Festival (Istanbul)	Classical	Jun-Jul
Istanbul Müzik Festival (Istanbul)	Classical/Jazz	Jun
Leyla Gencer Voice Competition (Istanbul)	Classical	Aug
Nuri Iyicil International Violin Competition (Istanbul)	Classical	Oct
Siemens Opera Competition (Istanbul)	Classical	Jan

FESTIVAL	GENRE	MONTH
United Kingdom		
Bestival (Isle of Wight, England)	Indie	Sep
Big Chill (Ledbury, England)	Electronic	Aug
Bloc Weekend (Butlins)	Electronic	Mar
Creamfields Festival (Cheshire, England)	Electronic	Aug
Glastonbury (Somerset, England)	Multi-Genre	Jun
Green Man (Brecon Beacons, Wales)	Folk/Psychedelia/Indie	Aug
Hinterland (Glasgow, Scotland)	Multi-Genre	Apr-May
Isle of Wight (Isle of Wight, England)	Rock/Alt Rock	Jun
Latitude Festival (Suffolk, England)	Alt/Punk/Indie Rock	Jul
Leeds Festival (Leeds)	Rock/Pop/Metal/Punk	Aug
Meltdown (London, England)	Multi-Genre	Jun
Reading Festival (Reading, England)	Rock/Pop/Metal/Punk	Aug
RockNess (Loch Ness, Scotland)	Rock/Alt Rock/Electronic/Hip-Hop	Jun
T in the Park (Balado, Scotland)	Alt Rock/Punk Rock/Electronic	Jul
V Festival (Chelmsford/Staffordshire)	Rock/Pop	Aug
United States & Canada		
All Points West (Jersey City, NJ)	Multi-Genre	Jul-Aug
Austin City Limits Festival (Austin, TX)	Rock/Pop	Sep-Oct
Bonnaroo (Manchester, TN)	Multi-Genre	Jun
Bumbershoot (Seattle, WA)	Rock/Pop	Sep
Chicago Jazz Festival (Chicago, IL)	Jazz	Sep
CMJ Music Marathon (New York, NY)	Multi-Genre	Oct
Coachella (Indio, CA)	Alt Rock/Hip-Hop/Electronic	Apr
Detroit Electronic Music Festival (Detroit, MI)	Electronic	May
Edgefest (Ann Arbor, MI)	Jazz	Oct
ESFNA Festival (Across North America)	Ethiopop	Jun-Jul
Festival International de Musique Actuelle de Victoriaville (Victoriaville, Canada)	Jazz/Contemporary	May
Joshua Tree Roots Music Festival (Joshua Tree, CA)	Folk/Roots	Oct
LA Acoustic Music Festival (Los Angeles, CA)	Folk/Roots	Jun
Lollapalooza (Chicago, IL)	Alt Rock/Punk/Hip-Hop	Aug
Mafrika Music Festival (New York, NY)	Ethiopop	Jun
Milwaukee Summerfest (Milwaukee, WI)	Multi-Genre	Jun-Jul
Monolith (Red Rocks Amphitheater, CO)	Rock/Pop	Sep
Monterey Jazz Festival (Monterey, CA)	Jazz	Sep
Musicfest NW (Portland, OR)	Rock/Pop	Sep
Mutek (Montreal, Canada)	Electronic	May-Jun
New Orleans Jazz Fest (New Orleans, LA)	Jazz/Country/Blues	Apr-May
Newport Jazz Fest (Newport, RI)	Jazz	Aug
Noise Pop (San Francisco, CA)	Indie	Feb-Mar
North by Northeast (Toronto, Canada)	Multi-Genre	Jun
Pitchfork (Chicago, IL)	Multi-Genre	Jul
Pop Montreal (Montreal, Canada)	Pop Rock	Sep-Oct
Sasquatch! (George, WA)	Alt Rock/Hip-Hop	May
Sheba Film Festival (New York, NY)	Ethiopop	May
Siren Music Festival (Brooklyn, NY)	Indie/Experimental Rock	Jul
South by Southwest (Austin, TX)	Multi-Genre	Mar

FESTIVAL	GENRE	MONTH
United States & Canada (cont'd)		
The Stagecoach Festivals (Indio, CA)	Folk/Roots	Apr
Umbrella Music Festival (Chicago, IL)	Jazz	Nov
Voodoo Experience (New Orleans, LA)	Multi-Genre	Oct
Vision Festival (New York, NY)	Jazz	Jun
Warped Tour (Throughout the United States and Canada)	Punk Rock/Metal/Electronic	Jun-Aug
West by Southwest (Tucson, AZ)	Multi-Genre	Mar
Winter Music Conference (Miami Beach, FL)	Electronic	Mar
XX Merge (Carrboro, NC)	Alternative	July
Worldwide		
All Tomorrow's Parties (England/ United States/Australia)	Post-Rock/Avant-Garde/ Underground Hip-Hop	Jan/May/Sep
WOMAD (All Over The World– 2009 was in Abu Dhabi/Spain/UK)	World Music/Rock/Jazz	Apr-Nov

(*Note: Dates subject to change. Some listings are based on previous editions. Check websites for possible updates.)

ACKNOWLEDGEMENTS

Photography for the Museyon Guides has been graciously provided by dozens of citizen photographers found through Flickr.com, our authors, featured artists, and venues. Museyon would like to thank them, as well as all the companies and photo libraries below:

flickr: 8, 11, 12, 13, 15, 17, 18, 19, 20, 25, 26, 27, 28, 29, 31, 36, 37, 41, 42, 43, 44, 45, 47, 48, 50, 52, 54, 57, 59, 60, 61, 63, 64, 65, 66, 67, 81, 103, 104, 106, 107, 109, 114, 119, 122, 130, 134, 137, 138, 142, 146, 147, 151, 154, 157, 162, 163, 167, 168, 170, 173, 176, 177, 180, 183, 186, 187, 188, 189,192, 193

istockphoto: 9, 25, 71, 77, 78, 103, 105, 109, 110, 111, 112, 119, 125, 128, 135, 147, 151, 153, 160, 167, 163, 191, 192,

shutterstock: 33, 41, 53, 73, 144, 152

Every effort has been made to trace and compensate copyright holders, and we apologize in advance for any accidental omissions. We would be happy to apply the corrections in the following edition of this publication.

CONTRIBUTORS

Mikael Awake grew up in Marietta, GA, where he would attend Ethiopian church services with his mother mainly to hear some dude wild out on the drum. He received a BA in English from Columbia University and is currently in the MFA creative writing program at Syracuse University. His work has appeared on Fader.com, McSweeney's Internet Tendency, and Monkeybicycle.net.

Shamik Bag's most recent professional stint has been as assistant editor with *Rolling Stone*'s Indian edition. Combining an obsessive interest in both music and travel, he has worked for the *Hindustan Times* and *Indian Express* newspapers and has written for *Mint, Outlook Traveller,* and *Travel + Leisure.*

Mel Campbell is a freelance journalist based in Melbourne, who was one of five idealistic fools behind the poster-magazine, *Is Not Magazine.* She was also deputy editor of the Australian monthly music magazine *jmag,* and in 2009, she co-founded the online pop-culture magazine, *The Enthusiast.*

Nick Frisch is a freelance journalist, consultant, and 2009–2010 Fulbright scholar, focusing on China's emerging music scenes. A New York City native, he has lived in Taipei, Hong Kong, and Beijing. He has written for *The Jewish Forward, South China Morning Post,* and *Il Giornale della Musica.*

James Hendicott's career in journalism began in South Korea, where he covered major events on behalf of Seoul Government Tourism and contributed to the entertainment section of the *Lonely Planet Seoul.* More recently he has been working for the Irish music magazine, *State.*

Eve Hyman spent her youth in Hollywood and then began writing about the arts and nightlife around her. Stretches in Italy, France, and New York City graduated to Buenos Aires, where restructured folklore, a raw street art scene, and a tumultuous political climate now lend inspiration. She has written for *Time Out Buenos Aires, Latina,* and *Urb* magazine.

Jessica Hundley is a writer and filmmaker living in LA. She has penned a travel guide to the City of Angels, a bio on country rock icon Gram Parsons, and has recently edited a book on Dennis Hopper's photography due out from Taschen in fall 2009.

Alexandra Ivanoff is a graduate of Yale University and the Eastman School of Music. She has had a multi-faceted career in New York and San Francisco as a performer in opera, musical theater, film and jazz, and also as a music publicist and agent. She currently resides in Istanbul and writes for *Time Out Istanbul* (English) and *Andante* music magazine (Turkish).

Peter Margasak is a staff writer with the *Chicago Reader*, where he covers all sorts of music. He is also a regular contributor to *Down Beat* magazine, where he authors the European Scene column.

Miles Marshall Lewis is a Bronx-born writer currently living in Paris with his wife and two sons. He is the author of *Scars of the Soul Are Why Kids Wear Bandages When They Don't Have Bruises* and *There's a Riot Goin' On.* He is also the founder and editor of the *Bronx Biannual* literary journal.

Siobhan O'Leary is a native New Yorker, who has worked for the publishing consulting firm, Market Partners International, and most recently, in the foreign rights department of the Crown Publishing Group. As a freelance writer, she has profiled clubs in Berlin, contributed to the travel guide *Inside New York*, and written for *Publishing Trends* and *Publishers Weekly*. She currently resides in Berlin.

Alina Simone is a singer and writer based in Brooklyn. Her latest album, *Everyone Is Crying Out to Me, Beware,* covered the music of Soviet punk poet Yanka Dyagileva and garnered praise from the BBC, *The New Yorker,* NPR and *SPIN*, among others. She is currently working on a collection of essays about Russia, family, and the tragic-comic struggle to make it in indie rock to be published by Faber in 2010.

ABOUT OUR ILLUSTRATOR

Jillian Tamaki is an illustrator from Calgary, Alberta, who now lives in Brooklyn, NY. In addition to her myriad editorial illustrations for publications such as *Entertainment Weekly, The New York Times*, and *SPIN,* she is also an award-winning graphic novelist. Co-authored alongside her cousin Mariko Tamaki, *Skim* was released in March 2008 and received the Ignatz Award for Best Graphic Novel.

ABOUT MUSEYON GUIDES

Museyon: A Curated Guide to Your Obsessions is a guidebook series that gives the curious subject a new and differently informed look at their interests. Based out of New York City with origins in Tokyo, Paris, and just about everywhere in between, Museyon is an independent publisher of quality information.